D

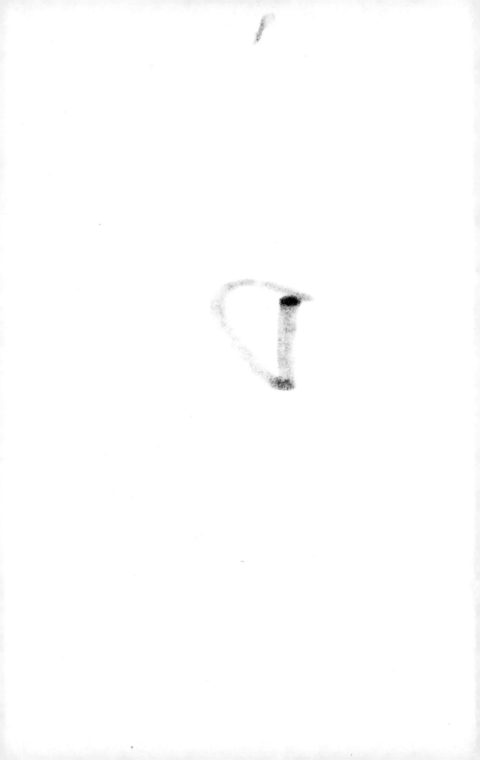

Rafael Palmeiro
At Home With the Baltimore Orioles

Ed Brandt

An Authorized Biography

Mitchell Lane Publishers, Inc.
P.O. Box 200
Childs, MD 21916-0200

RAFAEL PALMEIRO
AT HOME WITH THE BALTIMORE ORIOLES

The author and publisher wish to acknowledge with gratitude the help we received on this book from Fernando Cuza, José and Maria Palmeiro, and Lynne Palmeiro. They were patient with our never-ending requests for more information and photographs to make this book complete. Of course, our sincerest appreciation goes to Rafael, who took the time to talk with us through two baseball seasons when he would rather have been playing in the World Series. Parts of this book were based on contributing writer Barbara Marvis' personal interviews with Rafael.

First Printing

Library of Congress Cataloging-in-Publication Data

Brandt, Ed.
    Rafael Palmeiro: at home with the Baltimore Orioles: an authorized biography/Ed Brandt.
        p. cm.
    Includes index.
    ISBN 1-883845-37-8 (lib.) —ISBN 1-883845-38-6 (pbk.)
    1. Palmeiro, Rafael, 1964—   . 2. Baseball players—Biography. 3. Baltimore Orioles (Baseball team) I. Title.
GV865.P323B73 1998
796.357'092—dc21
[B]   97-8668
                                                                 CIP

TABLE OF CONTENTS

About the Author

Ed Brandt is a retired journalist with 45 years' experience as a sports writer and editor with the Baltimore *Sun* and the Norfolk *Virginian-Pilot*. He has published five previous books: **Last Voyage of the USS Pueblo** (1969, W.W. Norton), **When Hell Was in Session** (1977, Reader's Digest Press), **Fifty and Fired** (1987, Mills and Sanderson), **You and the Law** (1988, Media Materials), and **A Survey of World Cultures: Soviet Union** (1989, Media Materials). **When Hell Was in Session** became an NBC-TV movie in 1979.

Photograph Credits

p. 6 sketch by Barbara Tidman; pp. 8, 13, 21, 27, 35, 39, 40, 43, 48, 54 UPI/Corbis-Bettmann; p. 15 Archive Photos; p. 17 Ray Stubblebine/Reuters/Archive Photos; pp. 22, 24, 38, 42, 44, 46, 49, 50, 52, 68, 70, 78, 80, 87, 92, 94, 110 Jerry Wachter; pp. 56, 57, 58, 62, 121, 122 courtesy Maria and José Palmeiro; pp. 59, 60, 65, 66, 74, 75, 76, 118, 119, 120 courtesy Rafael and Lynne Palmeiro; pp. 89, 96 Joe Giza/Reuters/Archive Photos; p. 100 Mike Blake/Reuters/Archive Photos; p. 106 Globe Photos

INTRODUCTION
by Peter Angelos

When our investor group and I purchased the Baltimore Orioles franchise in October of 1993, our primary goal was to produce a championship team as soon as possible. We wanted to build a team with excellent athletes of high moral character, who played with intensity, and who would contribute to the community. In December of that year, we signed Rafael Palmeiro to a five-year contract worth approximately $30 million, then the highest price the franchise had ever paid for a player. I met with Rafael afterwards and he said, "You'll never be sorry for signing me, Mr. Angelos. I'll break my back for you."

I knew we had made the right choice, and I've never been disappointed. Rafael and I are on the same wavelength. I'm a perfectionist and he's a perfectionist. Our goal together has always been to bring a World Series championship to Baltimore regardless of personal sacrifice.

Rafael has produced handsomely on the field. He has been an intense, low-key performer, and a great one. More importantly, he is a highly principled man who sets the kind of moral standard that the Orioles must have. His charitable contributions are well known. Less known are his devotion to his family and his respect for the country he has adopted.

The Orioles to me are not just another baseball team. They are a symbol of our community's quest for excellence. The team provides entertainment for millions. It moderates the pain of our shut-ins. It affects the disaffected and brings them into our exciting world. It teaches our youth that there are better ways than the street.

That is the real Oriole magic, and I'm delighted that Rafael is a part of it.

Peter Angelos is a Baltimore attorney and majority owner of the Baltimore Orioles.

CHAPTER ONE
Cuba—My Homeland Rich in Baseball History

Baltimore Orioles manager Paul Richards walked slowly onto the field on a hot, dusty day in August 1960, waving his arms frantically and shouting at the home plate umpire to call time out.

The stage for this theatrical performance was old Griffith Stadium in Washington, D.C., home of the Washington Senators, the perennial last-place finishers in the American League, who at the moment were leading the Orioles 1–0 in the sixth inning of a game the pennant-contending Orioles needed to win.

The object of his anger was a baseball in the hand of umpire William McKinley, who stared bemused as Richards approached the plate insisting that the Washington pitcher, Camilo Pascual, was cutting the ball with something to make it miss the Orioles bats. This was an old trick. A pitcher would conceal a file or nail in his sleeve or elsewhere and nick the ball to make it spin in a way unfamiliar to batters, therefore creating an illegal and usually unhittable pitch. Pascual, a 26-year-old pitcher born in Havana, Cuba, and then in his seventh year with the Senators, really didn't need tricks to send disgusted Orioles batters back to the dugout one after the other, and everyone knew it, including Richards.

"I just wanted to throw Pascual off stride, break up his rhythm," Richards confessed after the game. "He was just mowing us down."

Richards' ploy didn't work. Pascual pitched a three-hitter, and the weak-kneed Senators won the game 2–0.

Paul Richards, right, is shown here with Casey Stengel in this 1960 photo. They are discussing pitching techniques. Richards died in 1986.

Pascual was typical of the Cuban players who had come north in the late 1940s and 1950s to play major league baseball. They were lean, tough and durable players who spoke English poorly if at all, but they did their talking

on the field with skillful play. They were Rafael Palmeiro's baseball ancestors, and they themselves were merely carrying on a tradition of Cuban baseball stretching back even before the founding of the National League in America in 1876. Cubans were playing organized baseball long before Colonel Teddy Roosevelt and his Rough Riders charged up San Juan Hill in 1898 during the Spanish-American War, a conflict that resulted in the liberation of Cuba from Spanish dominance.

In an article in a 1993 edition of the *Yale Law Review,* Robert Gonzalez Echevarria wrote about what is commonly considered the first baseball game played in Cuba. It was played on December 27, 1874, in Matanzas, a seaport on the northwestern coast of Cuba and about 75 miles east of Havana.

Echevarria doubts that this was actually the first game, but it was the first game covered by a writer in Cuba, thus giving it a certain signature that remains to this day. The writer, an aspiring author, chronicled the game between the home team, Matanzas, and the Habana Baseball Club. He noted that a "rhubarb" broke out shortly after the game began, with Habana charging the Matanzas pitcher with "throwing" the ball instead of "pitching" it.

Shades of Paul Richards!

In any case, the matter was settled, and Habana went on to demolish the home team 51–9. The game was notable for two things: Esteban Bellan hit two home runs for Habana, and Matanzas became the center of early Cuban baseball.

Bellan was the first Cuban player to compete in an American major league, going north for the 1871–73 seasons to play shortstop and third base for the New York Mutuals of the short-lived National Association. He batted .248 over the three seasons, but alas, no homers.

Christopher Columbus, when he discovered Cuba in 1492, called it "the loveliest land that human eyes have beheld." Matanzas province is one of its loveliest parts and was once one of its most prosperous because of the lush sugarcane fields that grew in its fertile soil. The port of Matanzas was once called the Athens of Cuba because of its wealthy, well-educated, and cosmopolitan population, which began thriving after the collapse of the sugar industry on the Caribbean island of Haiti in the early 1800s. The Havana elite, searching for fertile land, pushed eastward to Matanzas, where they bought land, built sugar mills, and used slave labor to work in the sugarcane fields. (Slavery was not abolished in Cuba until 1896.) Eventually, they began sending their sons to the United States to be educated, and among other things these sons brought back was—you guessed it—baseball. These sons organized the first Cuban baseball team in Matanzas, but this was not the only way that baseball reached Cuba.

Cuba had a lively trade with the United States, and American businessmen, merchant seamen, sailors from U.S. warships, and students spread the game throughout the island country. By the middle 1870s, it provided entertainment on warm Sundays for the population, which treated each game as a social affair. Eventually baseball became Cuba's national sport.

Baseball came along at a good time for the Cuban spirit, crushed during the first war of independence with Spain, which ended after ten years in 1878 with defeat for the rebels. It also provided an avenue between classes of people. The rich mingled with the poor during the games, and a good shortstop was as popular as anyone, whether he had a peso in his pocket or not. A young man's skills as a baseball player often opened doors that had been closed to him.

Baseball was not popular with the Spanish authorities who ruled the island. Several players were imprisoned because money raised at some games was given to the Cuban independence movement. The authorities viewed baseball as being played by revolutionaries. They also felt it was dangerous to the Spanish regime because it required the use of "sticks" (bats).

Eventually, leagues were formed, and after Cuban independence was achieved, when American forces defeated the Spanish in 1898, baseball began its march into its golden age in Cuba. It provided liberation of sorts for the young men who toiled in the sugarcane fields and mill towns of the country. Many of these young men became celebrities in their hometowns; and as towns, companies, and even politicians sponsored teams, the players gained nationwide fame.

Furthermore, Cuba became the father of baseball in and around the Caribbean. As Rob Ruck writes in **Total Baseball, the Ultimate Encyclopedia of Baseball,** the sport spread rapidly from Cuba to Mexico, Nicaragua, the Dominican Republic, Venezuela, Puerto Rico, Panama, and Colombia. "There was a fascination approaching reverence for baseball in the Caribbean," Ruck writes. "Baseball provided a common ground for everyone, it spoke a language all understood. It vented social tensions, and gave [the people] a sense of pride and accomplishment."

Baseball became part of the social fabric of these countries, and indeed it drew increasing interest from American professional teams. By the 1930s, American professionals, especially black players barred from the major leagues because of racial prejudice, found a hearty welcome in the Caribbean. Such future Hall of Famers as Josh Gibson, Cool Papa Bell, Luis Tiant Sr., and Satchel Paige were able to earn money during the winter months when the American Negro leagues were shut down.

The Cuban Stars, a team made up of players too dark-skinned to pass the major leagues' color line, barnstormed in the U.S. in the years before World War II, and many Cuban players joined the Negro leagues.

But there were Cubans light-skinned enough to make it to the majors. Adolfo Luque pitched in the American big leagues for twenty seasons, and in 1923 was 27 and 8 for the Washington Senators. Clark Griffith, the penny-pinching owner of the Senators, knew a good thing when he saw it. He sent Joe Cambria, a Cuban, to scout the island for promising players. Griffith liked the idea that he could get them cheaply, and the players had a certain quality of endurance and skill that made them stand out.

The Senators for two decades were a gateway to the United States for Cuban players, and Cambria became famous in baseball circles as a crafty and perceptive judge of talent. Camilo Pascual was one of his finds.

Major league teams had played exhibition games in Cuba as early as 1900, and later they began sending their young players to the Caribbean winter leagues for training and experience. They still do this, but not to Cuba.

Major league teams began canceling their exhibition games in Cuba in 1960, after

Satchel Paige, pitching for the Kansas City Monarchs in this 1942 photograph, was said to be the highest paid African American ball player at the time.

they caught on to Fidel Castro's intentions, with a nudge from the U.S. State Department. Castro had taken control of Cuba in early 1959, but it wasn't clear for nearly a year that he was setting up a Communist dictatorship. The Baltimore Orioles were about to board a plane for Havana in February 1960 when word came for them to go elsewhere. They went to Puerto Rico instead.

Castro, once a pretty good left-handed pitcher himself, effectively ended the flow of Cuban players to the U.S. when he took over the country. However, he has retained a keen interest in baseball. He pitched in an exhibition game for the Cuban army team as a sort of effort to show he was still one of the guys, and he allegedly struck out two batters in one inning. After the second strikeout, it is said, he rushed to the plate and shook hands with the umpire.

Baseball in Cuba is now only a tool of the revolution, and the only Cuban players directly from Cuba are defectors who have sought political asylum in the United States. Among these defectors are pitcher Ariel Prieto, whom the Los Angeles Dodgers believe will develop into a star; pitcher Osvaldo Fernandez of the San Francisco Giants; pitcher Livan Hernandez of the Florida Marlins; and Rey Ordonez, a shortstop for the New York Mets.

There is a powerful incentive for defection. Hernandez received a $4.5 million contract from the Marlins, and Fernandez got a $3.9 million deal from the Giants.

In July, 1996, prior to the Olympic Games in Atlanta, Rolando Arrojo, the Cuban national team's number one starting pitcher, made the "hard decision" to defect, leaving his wife and two children behind in Cuba. Arrojo, who led Cuba to victory over the U.S. Olympic team in an exhibition game in June, had been training with teammates in Albany, Georgia, in advance of the Olympics. Arrojo, 32, said: "I'm a little unhappy right now. I'm sorry I didn't tell my teammates, but it was a very personal decision and I had to make it myself. I had to make it to achieve my dream of personal freedom and playing in the major leagues."

Osvaldo Fernandez, a native of Holguin, Cuba, defected from the Cuban national team. He signed a three-year $3.9 million deal with the San Francisco Giants.

Arrojo, a 6-foot-4 right-hander, dominated the U.S. team in the June exhibition game. He pitched seven innings and kept the U.S. lineup of heavy hitters off stride with a variety of off-speed pitches. He scattered five hits and struck out seven.

The Olympic Games showed the quality of contemporary Cuban baseball. Despite losing some of their top pitchers to defection, the Cuban team squashed the opposition and won its second straight Olympic gold medal.

The players approached the Olympics with great confidence to the point of arrogance. "They expected to win every game," said U.S. Olympic coach Skip Bertman, and they did.

The U.S. team was supposed to be the main contender for the title, but the Cubans handed the Americans their first loss, 10–8, and Japan knocked the U.S. out of gold medal contention a couple of days later. The U.S. finished third, good for a bronze medal.

The championship game between Cuba and Japan was a wild one, with the lead swinging back and forth on the strength of 11 home runs before Cuba prevailed 13–9. Omar Linares, Cuba's gifted third baseman, hit three home runs in the final game; in his nine Olympic games, he hit eight homers, drove in 16 runs, and had a .476 batting average. Considered the world's top amateur player, he was offered a $1.5 million bonus in 1995 to sign with the New York Yankees, but he turned it down.

The Olympic medals were awarded a half hour after the game, and hardly a soul of the 44,000 who had attended had left the park. As the Cubans were draped with medals and handed flowers, they snapped pictures of one another and smiled widely. According to Cuban accounts, the team had won its 143rd straight international tournament game.

There were political sidelights to Olympic baseball, of course. Besides the defections, there was the sight of a curious blend of pro- and anti-Castro fans, both sides waving the Cuban flag, during the Cuba-U.S. game.

New York Mets runner, Rey Ordonez scores past Los Angeles Dodgers catcher Mike Piazza, June 1, 1996 at New York's Shea Stadium. Ordonez is a Cuban defector.

"The only reason this game is even close is because the U.S. bought Cuba's top pitchers," said a Castro supporter.

Said a U.S. fan: "These teams [U.S. and Cuba], are not comparable. We're a bunch of college kids playing older men and professionals."

Camilo Pascual, with his quick mind, quiet demeanor, and sharp curveball, was a role model for the many Cuban players who entered the major leagues in the 1950s. The Havana native was only 20 years old when he joined the Senators in 1954, and he was only 28 and 66 in his first five years with the American League's biggest losers.

But his record turned around in 1959, when he won 17 games and lost only 10. In the next six years, he was a 20-game winner three times and made the American League All-Star team three times. He finished his baseball career in Cleveland at age 37 with a 174–170 lifetime won-lost record.

His teammates, who called him "Little Potato," regarded him as a quiet but tough competitor who minded his own business but was somewhat superstitious. He wouldn't allow his picture to be taken on a day he was to pitch.

He also had a sharp wit. One day a reporter called him in his hotel room early in the morning and asked him if he spoke English.

"Not at seven o'clock in the morning," he said and hung up.

Pascual roomed with and palled around with another young Cuban pitcher named Pedro Ramos, who was born in Pinas del Rio, Cuba, and joined the Washington Senators in 1955 at the age of 20. Ramos started with the Senators at $6,500 a season, mere pocket change for today's players but a fortune for a young Cuban just out of the cane fields. Ramos was crazy about cowboy movies (he and Pascual would see two or three movies a day when they were on the road), and he liked to dress the part, striding around town in spurs, boots, and a cowboy hat.

Joe Cambria, the scout who had signed him, said he was "too pretty to be in baseball," and Ramos admitted that he had more girlfriends than he could handle. "I learned English in the minor leagues taking girls to the movies. They would translate for me," he said.

Perhaps the most colorful Cuban player of all was a Havana native, Orestes (Minnie) Minoso, who took the American League by storm when he was traded by Cleveland to the famous go-go Chicago White Sox in 1951. The White Sox were noted for their speed and zest for baseball, and, at the age of 27, Minoso fit right in.

When Jackie Robinson broke the major league color barrier in 1947 with the Brooklyn Dodgers, Minoso was still knocking around in the Cuban leagues and cutting sugarcane in the off-season. He was signed by the Indians in 1949 and spent most of the next two years in the minors.

The trade to the White Sox started Minoso on a 16-year tear in the majors, where he hit with power, played the outfield with great skill, and became a terror on the base paths, leading the league in steals three straight years in the early 1950s. He was American League rookie of the year in 1951.

Minoso, a fancy dresser and wit who used to argue with the umpires in Spanish, had a lifetime batting average of .298, when major league pitching was much tougher than it is today. He hit 186 home runs and stole 205 bases before ending his career in 1976.

The 1950s were a difficult time for black players. A few white players were resentful and feared they would lose their jobs to black players. Jackie Robinson endured numerous insults and physical assaults on the playing field, but he took them without emotion, letting his skills do his talking. Segregation was still in force in many parts of the country, and black and white players stayed in separate hotels well into the 1960s.

The word Colored used to be written on the passports of black players. When a man tried to write the word on Minoso's passport, he snatched it away. "Don't write that colored stuff on my passport. I'm Cuban," he said. But mostly, Minoso was too good-natured to be riled by such things. When a player once remarked about his dark color, Minoso smiled and said, "You don't look so good yourself."

Cuba has produced many powerhouse players for the major leagues. Luis Tiant, a styl-

ish pitcher with a baffling windup, pitched for nineteen years—from 1964 to 1982—with Cleveland, Boston and New York and won 229 games.

Mike Cuellar, Connie Moreno and Sandy Consuegra were highly successful pitchers from Cuba. Tony Oliva, from Pinar Del Rio, spent fifteen years (1962–76) with the Minnesota Twins and led the American League in hits five of those years. He was rookie of the year in 1962 and played in seven All-Star games.

A native Cuban currently in the majors is slugger José Canseco, who was born in Havana. And there have been many other outstanding players from the island in the Caribbean who have made a lasting mark in the American major leagues.

This 1971 photo of the Orioles pitchers includes (from left to right): Jim Palmer, Dave McNally (rear), Pat Dobson, and Mike Cuellar.

CHAPTER TWO
The Baltimore Orioles
How They Came to Be

Peter G. Angelos officially arrived on the Baltimore baseball scene in October 1993, when he and twenty partners bought the club at auction for a then baseball record franchise cost of $173 million after its owner went bankrupt. The sale not only bailed former owner Eli Jacobs out of bankruptcy (he made a cool $100 million on the deal), but it brought Peter Angelos to the helm of one of the most famous franchises in baseball, with a history going back to the 1870s.

As the team's managing general partner, Angelos brings special assets: he is energetic, he pledged to make the Orioles a winner, and he is rich, having made millions litigating lawsuits on behalf of workers exposed to asbestos. He started making good on his pledge to create a winner when he signed first baseman Rafael Palmeiro, after five days of intense negotiation, to a five-year, $30 million contract to begin in the 1994 season.

Peter Angelos vowed to make the Baltimore Orioles a winning team when he and twenty other investors purchased the franchise in 1993.

"I'm delighted to go to the Orioles," Palmeiro said. "I'm not going there to be Superman. I'm going there to do what I've always done—be consistent, play every day, and do everything I can to win."

Anyone with any sense of Orioles history—and there are many in Baltimore who know the history inside and out—might think back to the early days of the Orioles and their first great first baseman, Big Dan Brouthers. Brouthers played only two of his seventeen major league seasons for the Orioles, but they were championship years, and in 1894 he slugged 23 home runs in the days when home runs were much harder to come by than they are now.

The Orioles had been a member of various minor leagues in the 1880s. They moved up to the major leagues in 1892 when they joined the 12-team National League. They were owned by a colorful character named Harry Von Der Horst, a prosperous Baltimore beer maker who sold thousands of gallons of his product at Orioles games. At one point, when his team was doing badly, the portly owner said, "We don't win many baseball games, but we sell lots of beer!"

The Orioles finished last in its first season in the National League, but then Von Der Horst brought in a tough, scrappy manager named Ned Hanlon. Hanlon changed the game of baseball forever.

Hanlon was a stern, demanding manager who would not let anyone meddle with his team. Just to make it clear who was running the Orioles, Von Der Horst began wearing a button on his lapel that said, "Ask Hanlon."

Hanlon kept infielder John McGraw, who later became a famous manager of the New York Giants, and catcher Wilbert Robinson, but he got rid of most of the rest of the team. He brought in Brouthers and wispy Wee Willie Keeler, an outfielder who was only 5 foot 4 and weighed a mere 135 pounds. Keeler hit for an astonishingly high average, including .424 in 1898. When asked how he did it, he replied in words that would immortalize him in baseball history: "Hit 'em where they ain't."

Hanlon created "scientific baseball," which emphasized the bunt and the hit-and-run, where the base runner would take off with the pitch and the batter would swing at whatever came plateward. He showed them how to do the famous Baltimore chop. The batter would fake a bunt, then smash the ball into the ground, making it bounce so high in the air that he could beat the throw to first.

The new lineup that Hanlon fielded in 1894 included six future Hall of Famers: Brouthers; shortstop Hughie Jennings; McGraw; outfielder Joe Kelley; Keeler; and Robinson. More than 15,000 wildly cheering fans packed the 6,000-seat Union Park to watch the Orioles destroy the New York Giants in a doubleheader on opening day, with half the crowd lining the outfield and clogging the aisles to watch the games.

The Orioles were slick in all departments of the game and were so tough that opposing players and owners complained constantly about their rough play. Orioles players would stomp the feet of opposing players with their spikes, go out of their way to knock down infielders while running the base paths, and take the field with bandages covering their cut hands

John McGraw (left) shown here with Rogers Hornsby in 1927, became a famous manager of the New York Giants.

27

and skinned arms to enhance their tough image.

"They were mean, vicious, ready at any time to maim a rival player or an umpire if it helped their cause," one umpire complained.

The Orioles swept to three straight National League pennants (1894, '95, and '96) and won the Temple Cup, the 1890s version of the World Series between the first and second place finishers, all three times. But by 1898, when Hanlon became manager of the Brooklyn Dodgers and the baseball power shifted to that city, the team began to come apart. Attendance fell sharply, and the National League dropped the Orioles for the 1900 season. Orioles fans were stunned. The greatest team in the short history of the major leagues was gone. The Orioles played in the newly formed American League in 1901, but they finished last in 1902, and the franchise was shifted to New York. That franchise became the New York Highlanders, and later the Yankees.

The Orioles, named after the Baltimore Oriole, a slim, shy bird native to the region, spent the next 52 years in the minors, most of that time in the International League, a league just a small cut below the two major leagues, but a minor league nonetheless. However, there were some remarkable developments that made the Orioles' long tenure in the minors endurable.

The first of these events was the arrival in Baltimore of Jack Dunn, a tall, slight former pitcher with a penetrating, high-pitched voice who took over as manager and owner of the Orioles in 1907. Dunn was an excellent manager, but most of all he had an aptitude for spotting and developing raw baseball talent. He was the savior of Baltimore baseball as he turned the Orioles into one of the most successful and storied franchises of all time.

The Orioles finished sixth in 1907, but they came back the next year to win the first of the nine International League championships they would capture under Dunn's leadership. Dunn was an expert at developing talent, and he operated profitably by selling young stars to the majors for then princely sums, including two Baltimore natives, brothers Fritz and George Maisel. Third baseman Fritz Maisel stole 74 bases for the New York Yankees in 1913, setting a major league record.

In 1914, Dunn made his greatest deal. A priest at St. Mary's Industrial School, an institution for wayward boys run by a Catholic brotherhood, told Dunn he had an immensely talented player on the St. Mary's baseball team, a nineteen-year-old named George Herman Ruth. Dunn watched Ruth play and came away astonished at Ruth's raw ability.

Ruth had been placed in St. Mary's by his father, a saloon keeper whose Ruth's Family Saloon is now somewhere under the center-field sod at Baltimore's new Camden Yards ballpark. He felt his son had become unmanageable.

The youngster, with his huge hands and aggressive personality, was the best pitcher Dunn had ever seen at any age. Furthermore, Ruth, known by his St. Mary's teammates as Babe, could hit the ball out of sight.

The brothers insisted that Dunn adopt Babe Ruth, making him a ward of the Orioles owner until he reached 21 years of age. Dunn agreed. He gave him a $600 signing bonus and put him on a train for spring training. Ruth struck out Hall of Famers like Home Run Baker and Eddie Collins during exhibition games, and he started the 1914 season as a regular.

By midseason Ruth had won 13 games and lost 8, and several major league teams became interested in him. Despite their success on the field, the Orioles were in financial trouble, and Dunn reluctantly sold Ruth to the Boston Red Sox for $2,900.

Ruth was not popular with the Boston players, who resented his taking batting practice even though he was a pitcher. He came to the park one day and found his bats sawed neatly in half. Ruth pitched and won the first major league game he ever saw, beating Cleveland 4–3, on July 11, 1914. He led the Red Sox to the American League pennant in 1915 with an 18 and 6 record. He also hit five home runs.

The Red Sox won the pennant again in 1916 and also won the World Series. Ruth received a $4,000 World Series check and bought an 80-acre farm outside of Boston. But his stay in Boston was short-lived. A man named Harry Frazee, a theatrical producer and fight promoter and a well-known man about town, bought the

Red Sox after the 1916 season for $675,000. "I have always enjoyed baseball," Frazee said, "and now I have a chance to show what I know about handling a baseball club."

As he was shortly to prove, he didn't know anything about handling a baseball club, except for one matter. He asked Ruth to play every day. He would play the outfield when he wasn't pitching, and Frazee raised his salary from $5,000 to $7,000 a year in 1918. The Red Sox made it to the World Series again, beating the Cubs in six games. Ruth pitched a shutout in the opener and set a World Series record that still stands by extending his scoreless-inning string to 29 innings.

The Red Sox have not won a World Series since, much to the despair of Boston fans, who still blame Harry Frazee for the debacle that followed.

The Red Sox slipped to sixth place in 1919, despite Ruth's record 29 home runs and 114 runs batted in, 20 percent of Boston's total for the year. Ruth was now making $10,000 a year, but he wasn't satisfied and was giving Frazee trouble over his salary. Frazee decided to put Ruth up for sale, and on December 26, 1919, he sold the slugger to the New York Yankees for $100,000 and a $300,000 loan, stunning the baseball world and setting the Yankees on the path to a baseball dynasty that continues to this day.

As Dan Shaughnessy notes in his book, **The Curse of the Bambino,** Boston fans still feel cursed by the sale and believe the Red Sox's more than 75 years in the baseball desert comes directly from that fateful sale.

The rest is history. Babe Ruth became an idol of baseball fans all over the world during the 1920s and '30s. He hit 714 home runs in a 22-year major league career, and in 1927 hit an astounding 60 home runs. His 714 home runs stood as a record until Hank Aaron broke it in 1974, eventually hitting a career 755 home runs. Roger Maris broke Ruth's single-season record in 1961 with 61 homers, but he did it after the American League season was extended from 154 to 162 games.

Meanwhile, Jack Dunn was preparing his International League Orioles for Baltimore's Golden Age in minor league baseball. By 1919, he had assembled a talented team through his own ability to spot talent and develop it.

The Orioles, now playing in Oriole Park at Greenmount Avenue and 29th Street, became a focal point for the baseball-hungry fans, and they swarmed to the park to see the Orioles win 100 games and the International League pennant, the first of seven straight championships. It is a record that has never been matched at any level of professional baseball.

The Orioles gave their fans their money's worth, producing such fine players as Joe Boley, Fritz Maisel, Max Bishop, George Earnshaw, Johnny Ogden, and Jack Bentley, all of whom went on to major league stardom.

Then there was Lefty Grove, the great left-handed pitcher from Lonaconing, Maryland. He won 108 games for the Orioles in four and a half years before Dunn sold him to the Philadelphia Athletics for the then incredible price of $100,000. Grove went on to win 300 games for the A's and the Boston Red Sox and was voted into the Baseball Hall of Fame.

The Orioles' championship string ended with the 1926 season, and in 1928, Jack Dunn died at the age of 58 of pneumonia after a fall off a horse. The Orioles slumped into mediocrity after Dunn's death and didn't win another International League pennant until 1944. But Baltimore fans still loved them. On warm Sunday afternoons, thousands of fans would take the No. 8 streetcar to Oriole Park and watch the Orioles play a doubleheader against the Jersey City Giants, the Montreal Royals, or the hated Newark Bears, a farm club of the New York Yankees. The stands would be filled with men in flat-topped, brimmed straw hats, the male headgear of the 1920s and 1930s, drinking beer and cheering such sluggers as Buzz Arlett, Joe Hauser, Howie Moss, and George Puccinello. Afterward, many of them would retire to a local saloon for more beer and a crabcake or two.

On one warm Sunday afternoon, the Orioles were playing the Syracuse Chiefs in a close ball game. The score was tied, 1–1, in the tenth inning. A portly fan was sitting on the steps of an aisle with his ten-year-old son (the stands were packed and spectators lined the outfield for this important game) when Puccinello, a big right-handed hitter, came to the plate to lead off for the Orioles. The fan nudged his son and said, "He's going to hit a home run." The boy watched in amazement as Puccinello hit the first pitch high over the left field wall.

In 1944, the Orioles, now owned by Jack Dunn III, Jack Dunn's grandson, put together a marvelous season of comeback victories to win the International League pennant and the Junior World Series against Louisville. But that wasn't the most important thing that happened to Orioles baseball that year. On July 4, something occurred that led directly to Baltimore's eventual return to the major leagues. Oriole Park burned down to the last seat, and the Orioles were forced to move to Municipal Stadium, a ramshackle football stadium that seated 80,000 people. The stadium was renovated for baseball, and for one game during the Junior World Series, 52,833 fans attended. On that same day, game six of the major league World Series, played in St. Louis, drew only 31,000 fans. This astonishing event opened the eyes of baseball people and marked Baltimore for a return to the big leagues. Clark Griffith, owner of the Washington Senators, opposed a franchise for Baltimore because he feared the Orioles would draw fans from Washington, only 45 miles away. It took several more years for Baltimore's dream to be realized.

The fight for a franchise was led by Roger Pippin, crusty sports editor of the Baltimore *News Post*, who badgered the public to spend $2.5 million to rebuild Municipal Stadium for baseball, then kept the heat on political and civic leaders to bring major league baseball to Baltimore. Finally, shortly after the 1953 season ended, a Baltimore group led by attorney Clarence Miles paid Bill Veeck, the owner of the St. Louis Browns, nearly $2.5 million for the franchise. Major league baseball was back in Baltimore.

Unfortunately, the tattered Browns came with the franchise. The Browns had finished in the first division of the American League only 13 times in 52 years and had won only one pennant. The lineup that came to Baltimore was a disaster, and the Orioles lost 100

When Oriole Park burnt down in 1944, Baltimore's football stadium, Municipal Stadium below, was rebuilt for baseball and renamed Memorial Stadium.

of 154 games in 1954, their first year in the American League.

Two first basemen, Eddie Waitkus and Dick Kryhoski, came with the team, and thus became Rafael Palmeiro's distant Oriole ancestors at first. Waitkus was best known for being shot in the chest by a lunatic woman after she invited him to her hotel room. Kryhoski hit dozens of home runs foul, but only one fair in the 1954 season. Between them, the pair had three home runs.

The Orioles didn't have a representative first baseman until 1960, when they acquired handsome Diamond Jim Gentile, so named because of his flashy dress and his way with the ladies, from the Los Angeles Dodgers. Gentile slugged a career high 46 home runs and drove in an astounding 141 runs in 1961.

Gentile was followed at first base by burly Boog Powell, a mainstay on four championship teams, and Eddie Murray, who will someday be in baseball's Hall of Fame. So Palmeiro has a great challenge to meet as the Orioles' first baseman, a challenge he has so far met magnificently.

After the 1954 season, the Orioles hired Paul Richards, a lean, studious Texan, as manager and general manager. They gave him instructions to build the Orioles into a winner regardless of cost. Richards was a bona fide genius, well-read in the classics, a student of baseball, a keen judge of talent, and deeply knowledgeable in the psychology of baseball. As an example, he once had a strong left-handed pitcher, named Steve Barber, who was having problems getting the ball over the plate. Richards was sitting in the dugout one day studying Barber's delivery. He turned to a sportswriter and said, "Barber has a hitch in his delivery that makes the ball come in high." The sportswriter asked Richards why he didn't tell him that. "Well, he won't listen," Richards said. "Have to wait until he gets in trouble this season. Then he'll come to me and ask what's wrong, and I'll tell him and he'll listen." That's exactly what happened, and Barber went on to become a star pitcher, winning 20 games for the Orioles in 1963.

Richards was a patient man who knew that the best path to a winner was a strong farm system. He expanded the scouting program and installed veteran managers in the minor league system, instructing them to stress pitching and defense and baseball basics. His philosophy served the Orioles for many years, even after he left the team in 1961.

Richards had a certain grand style about him and a droll sense of humor, as Ted Patterson notes in his book, **The Baltimore Orioles.** Early in his tenure, he told the sportswriters, "Some day, boys, maybe four or five years from now, Baltimore will have a fine young team on the field. When that day finally comes, and a pennant is hoisted on the Stadium flagpole, all I ask is that you observe a moment of silence in memory of old No. 12."

Richards' first great score on the road to fulfilling his promise was to sign Brooks Robinson on May 30, 1955, two weeks after Robinson's eighteenth birthday, for a signing bonus of $4,000. The Little Rock, Arkansas, native was a second baseman in high school, but after watching Robinson play, Richards said, "That boy might just become the greatest third baseman who ever lived." After two years of switching from the Orioles to the minors and back again, Robinson became an Oriole regular

Brooks Robinson was an Orioles bonus baby, signed in 1955.

Diamond Jim Gentile, left, was driving in many runs for the Orioles in the 1961 season.

John "Boog" Powell, bottom left, was safe at home after the Minnesota Twins' pitcher Pete Cimino dropped the throw from catcher Earl Battey in this 1966 photograph.

at third base in 1958. He was inducted into the Hall of Fame in 1983.

Richards gradually built the Orioles into a pennant contender. The team led the American League in 1960 as late as September before falling back and finishing third. Gentile was driving in runs like crazy, including a double-grand-slam night against Minnesota in 1961, and the pitching staff Richards had developed was superb. But Richards left after the 1961 season to become general manager of Houston, the new National League expansion team, and the Orioles began to stumble.

The Orioles got batting instructions from Manager Paul Richards on their first day of spring training in March 1960.

Richards, however, had left a great legacy after seven years with the Orioles. He had constructed a solid farm system that began to feed good young players to the parent team, and his visions of greatness became reality when the

Orioles produced the best record in baseball over the next quarter century.

One day in 1961, at the Orioles' spring training home park in Miami, a man named Larry MacPhail was sitting in the stands watching the pregame warm-up. MacPhail was one of the famous baseball men of the day. He owned the New York Yankees and was regarded as a keen judge of talent. He watched a burly, overweight player taking fly balls in the outfield.

"That fellow," he said, pointing his finger, "will make a great baseball player if the knife and fork doesn't get him."

Boog Powell never stopped eating (his playing weight was 230 pounds, a lot for those days of smaller players), but this didn't stop him from becoming a great first baseman and another long link to the present day and Rafael Palmeiro.

Powell switched between the outfield and first base until the 1966 season when he became the regular first baseman. For 14 seasons, he hammered home runs and drove in runs for the Orioles, including 39 home runs in 1964. That was tops for the Orioles until Palmeiro came along and hit a matching 39 home runs in 1995 and 1996. Powell now operates a popular barbecue stand behind the right field wall at Camden Yards.

By 1966, Richards' vision for the Orioles had begun to pay off. They had pitching and defense, and after the 1965 season they acquired a player who would make them

Boog Powell operates a popular barbeque stand at Camden Yards. He is always available to sign autographs and chat with fans.

champions. Frank Robinson had played ten seasons with the Cincinnati Reds, hitting 324 home runs and driving in more than 1,000 runs, and the Orioles gave up a good pitcher, Milt Pappas, and a couple of throw-ins to get him.

Robinson was the catalyst that made the Orioles work, but he had plenty of support, including Boog Powell and future Hall of Famers Brooks Robinson and Jim Palmer, who was only

19 years old when he broke in with the Orioles in 1965.

Frank Robinson got everyone's attention on May 9, 1966, including that of the new Orioles owner Jerry Hoffberger, when he became the first and only player to hit a ball out of Memorial Stadium. It was measured at 540 feet from home plate and came off Cleveland pitcher Luis Tiant, a Cuban from Marianao, Cuba, whose sparkling 19-year major league career included 229 victories.

The Orioles moved into first place to stay on June 21 and won the American League pennant by nine games. They were given little chance to defeat the fearsome Los Angeles Dodgers, winners of the National League pennant. The Dodgers were led by 27-game winner

Frank Robinson (left) and Brooks Robinson (right) became heroes of the first World Series game on October 5, 1966, when each hit a home run in the first inning off Don Drysdale to give the Orioles all the margin they needed for the win. They are shown here in the Orioles dressing room.

Frank Robinson was the first and only player to hit a ball out of Memorial Stadium. It was measured at 540 feet from home plate!

Sandy Koufax, but the Orioles swept them in four straight games, the last three being complete game shutouts by Palmer, Wally Bunker, and Dave McNally.

It was the beginning of a glorious decade for the Orioles, who won American League pennants in 1969, '70, and '71, and the World Series in 1970 under future Hall of Fame manager Earl Weaver. They won the American League Eastern Division in 1973–74 but lost to the powerful Oakland Athletics in the playoffs both years.

Two milestones were passed in 1977 when Brooks Robinson retired and Eddie

Murray came up through the farm system to become the Orioles' first baseman. Murray hit 20 or more home runs for 12 years and led the Orioles to two American League pennants (1979 and 1983) and the 1983 World Series championship. Murray was later traded to the Los Angeles Dodgers and then to the Cleveland Indians. He came back to the Orioles in 1996 in time to hit the 500th home run of his glorious career.

There was another great player coming up to add to the Orioles' stellar list. He was shortstop Cal Ripken Jr., son of Orioles coach Cal Ripken. The Orioles drafted him on the second round of the 1978 draft, and, at the end of the 1981 season, after four years and 23 home runs at Rochester, the Orioles' farm team in the International League, he came up to the Orioles to stay.

At 6 feet 4 and 220 pounds, Ripken was considered too big to play shortstop in the majors, but he quickly demonstrated that he could do it. He had been the Oriole shortstop, starting in the 1982 season, until he was moved to third base for the 1997 season.

Ripken has hit for average and power in his long career and has been voted to the American League All-Star team 14 times. But most remarkable is his breaking of The Streak, Lou Gehrig's record of playing 2,130 straight games for the New York Yankees in the 1920s and '30s. It was a streak that was never supposed to have been broken in the modern age of base-

Cal Ripken Jr. played shortstop for the Orioles from the 1982 season until he was moved to third base for the 1997 season.

ball. But Ripken did it, tying Gehrig's record on September 6, 1995, and breaking it the next night in the new Oriole Park at Camden Yards, a moment baseball fans everywhere will never forget. Ripken continues to play every day, and

he will hold a record that will truly never be broken. By the end of the 1996 season, Ripken's streak had reached 2,153 games.

The Orioles began to go downhill after the 1983 season, which was the first for owner Edward Bennett Williams, a wealthy Washington attorney who had bought the team from Jerry Hoffberger for $12 million. By 1986, the team was a disaster. It finished last in its division, suffering its first losing season in 18 years, and in 1987, with Cal Ripken Sr. as manager, it finished sixth. When the Orioles started the 1988 season with 21 straight losses, Ripken was fired and replaced by Frank Robinson, but that didn't help. The Orioles won only 54 games and finished last again.

Owner Williams, eager to produce a winner, had defied the system that Paul Richards insisted was necessary for a winner. Richards had built the Orioles from the bottom up, through the farm system, but Williams had virtually ignored the farm system, pouring money into aging stars instead of the Orioles' minor league teams.

Williams had been gravely ill with cancer, and he died in August 1988. His estate sold the team to Eli Jacobs, a New York financier who was never popular with Orioles fans, for $70 million, then the second highest price ever paid for a baseball franchise.

Jacobs seemed more interested in entertaining his influential friends at the games than building a team, but the results he produced were not bad. In his five years as owner, the Orioles were in three pennant races almost to the end and broke attendance records in four of those years. He was also central to the planning and development of Oriole Park at Camden Yards, which set an industry standard for ball park design when it opened in 1992. It also set a standard for attendance, with huge crowds turning out every night for Orioles games. More than 3.6 million fans turned out in 1993 to crowd the 48,000-seat facility in downtown Baltimore. Unless you got your tickets early, they were very difficult to come by.

The Orioles' success didn't translate to Jacobs' personal bottom line, however, as his financial empire came apart. He failed to repay loans, his own $2.6 million home in Baltimore was foreclosed, and in April 1993 he declared bankruptcy. He had to sell the Orioles, and Pe-

The Baltimore Orioles played the New York Mets in an exhibition game at the new Oriole Park at Camden Yards, April 3, 1992.

ter Angelos immediately announced his intention to buy the club. But competing bidders, including a group from Cincinnati and a New York art dealer, soon showed up to vie for this valuable piece of property, and the franchise went on the auction block.

Earl Weaver (r) is the most winning manager in the history of the Baltimore Orioles. He is one of only 12 managers in big league history to have managed in four or more World Series.

The art dealer, Jeffrey Loria, stayed in to the bitter end, but Angelos told him, "I don't give a damn if it's $200 million. We're going to buy this ball club." Loria dropped out at the then record price of $173 million. The Orioles belonged to Angelos and his co-owners.

Angelos, then 64, had been a fan of the Orioles since their arrival in 1954. He put $40 million of his own money into the pot, with author Tom Clancy putting up $20 million as the next largest stockholder.

Angelos is an engaging, outspoken man who drives his own car, works 14-hour days, and eats lunch at his desk. He grew up in Highlandtown, a lower middle class section in East Baltimore where his Greek immigrant parents owned a bar. "He's tough as hell," said one

Orioles owner, Peter Angelos (front right) is shown here with author/investor Tom Clancy (left center) at an Orioles game. Angelos and Clancy attend many of the home games.

admirer. "He won't back down to anyone. He must've learned that in Highlandtown."

In the late 1970s, Angelos, an attorney, was in the forefront in litigating cases on behalf of workers who suffered from exposure to asbestos. He negotiated settlements or won damages totaling more than $1 billion, arguing many of the cases himself.

By the 1996 season, Angelos had increased the Orioles' player payroll to about $50 million and promised to spend more if that's what it took to create a winner.

He's still proud of his first big move as an owner: signing Rafael Palmeiro to play first base for the Orioles, thus extending a long line of great Oriole first basemen. It was a move that has paid off.

CHAPTER THREE
Rafael Palmeiro
At Home With the
Baltimore Orioles

T he long cold winter of 1994 was ended, but spring did not arrive in Baltimore until 3:17 P.M. on April 4, when pitcher Mike Mussina, under a bright blue sky, threw a strike past Kansas City Royals outfielder Vince Coleman to open the baseball season. A roaring crowd of 47,549 packed Camden Yards, home of the Baltimore Orioles, to watch their new-look team defeat the Royals 6–3. The centerpiece of their attention was the new first baseman, Rafael Palmeiro, signed as a free agent during the off-season to a five-year contract worth more than $30 million.

The signing was a step toward fulfilling Orioles owner Peter Angelos's pledge to bring a winner to Baltimore, and the festive crowd wasted no time in recognizing that the Havana-born Palmeiro was a major part of that pledge. They gave him a thunderous standing ovation when he appeared on the field for pregame warm-ups, then went absolutely wild after he hit a home run, a high, lazy drive into the right field bleachers, in the seventh inning.

Palmeiro shook hands with his teammates, stopped at the bottom of the dugout steps, then turned and looked back at the stands. The fans were still standing and cheering.

Palmeiro tips his cap to his roaring fans.

"What do they want?" he said to no one in particular. At the age of 29, he had been in the major leagues for six years, was a two-time All-Star, and had never been asked to make a curtain call.

"They want you," said manager Johnny Oates, "and they're not going to stop until they see you. This town is yours."

Palmeiro stepped to the top step of the dugout, waved his black cap in acknowledgment, then went back and sat on the bench, still smiling. He popped a large wad of chewing gum into his mouth, sat back, and sighed contentedly.

"The most special moment of my career," he said after the game. "I've never had fans make me feel special. I've had great games and ovations and all, but never anything like that. I'll never forget it. It makes me want to go out and play my butt off for them. I feel like today is the beginning of a good, long relationship."

It was a long way from there to here, but Palmeiro's skills and diligence have made the path easier to follow.

Rafael Corrales Palmeiro was born in Havana, Cuba, on September 24, 1964, the second of three sons of Maria and José Palmeiro. His father owned a concession stand, and the family was comfortable despite overriding poverty in the Caribbean island. But the parents thought opportunities for their children were limited, and they tried to move their family to the United States in 1963.

At first the Cuban government wouldn't allow them to emigrate, but by 1971 the political climate had changed and the family was permitted to leave. Unfortunately, they were not allowed to take any property with them. They arrived in Miami with only the clothes on their backs. José quickly found a job in the construction business, and the Palmeiros were on their way to a comfortable, middle-class existence in the United States.

Palmeiro was just starting first grade, and he was placed in a special class where the teachers spoke Spanish. "I hated school when I first started. It was a bad experience. I couldn't speak to anyone except the teachers, and I didn't know what anyone was talking about. When my mother came to wake me for school, I would pretend I didn't hear her. I cried every day.

Rafael with his brothers. From left to right: Rick, 8; André, 4; and Rafael, 7.

"When I finally learned the language, things became fun again. I had friends I could hang out with and talk to," he said.

Palmeiro was a good student despite his language difficulties. His favorite subject was math, and he also enjoyed sports. "I always liked to play sports in school, and by the time I was ten, I knew I loved baseball most of all. When people would ask me what I wanted to do when I grew up, I always told them I would be a baseball player, even though I didn't know what it would take at the time."

Rafael at 4 years old, taken in Cuba.

Millions of children want to play major league baseball, and his friends told Palmeiro it was a nice dream, but it was just a dream. He realized that it wouldn't be easy, and that only a small percentage of players ever make it to the major leagues. Even his father explained to him that the odds were against him and that he should think of a different career.

A person close to him said recently that the key to Palmeiro's success is in his personality. He has patience, and he is a perfectionist. As sweet as his swing with the bat might be, he has always searched for ways to make it better.

High school graduation, 1982

1981, playing ball for Miami Jackson High

"I was a good player all through school, and the older I got, the better I got," he said. "I really began to believe I would have a baseball career." This was the kind of determination and perseverance that would eventually make it happen.

Palmeiro played softball in junior high school and baseball at Miami Jackson High School. He got his high school diploma in 1982.

"If you do well in high school, the colleges send people around to see you play," he said. He not only played well, he excelled, and he was offered a full scholarship to play baseball at Mississippi State University in Starkville, a school noted for its excellent baseball teams.

He was also given the chance to play professional baseball after high school when he was drafted by the New York Mets in the eighth round of the free agent draft in June 1982. He wisely decided to forgo the opportunity for the chance to get a college education, and he enrolled at Mississippi State with a major in architecture. He later switched to a commercial art major because architecture was a complex subject and baseball was taking so much of his time.

At Mississippi State, he was a teammate of Will Clark, who played first base and who was later to play an important role in Palmeiro's career.

"My college years were a lot of fun," Palmeiro recalls. "Baseball was everything, and there were thirty or forty guys that I hung around with."

Rafael (center) with wife, Lynne and son Patrick traveled back to Mississippi State for a special appearance.

Palmeiro played in the outfield and was an All-American for two years. He won the Southeastern Conference triple crown in 1984, averaging .415 with 29 home runs and 94 runs batted in. The players had parties after most of the games, and it was at one of those parties in 1983 that he met Lynne Walden, who was enrolled at Mississippi State as a marketing major. They began to date.

At the end of his junior year, Palmeiro decided the time was right to become a professional baseball player. He was drafted by the Chicago Cubs in 1985, as a first-round choice, and he thought he should take the chance while he had it.

Rafael signed his first contract with the Chicago Cubs, June 1985.

"I figured my college degree would just sit in a drawer somewhere, and I had better take

the opportunity and sign with the Cubs," he said. In June 1985, he signed a Cub contract and soon was on the way to the minor leagues at $700 a month. In December of the same year, he and Lynne were married.

By the time he paid his $400-a-month rent, there wasn't much left to live on, but he was confident he would quickly move up through the minors to the major leagues—and the big money. He was right.

Palmeiro started out with the Cubs' Peoria, Illinois, Class A team in the Midwest League, one step above the very lowest Rookie League classification. He played in the outfield and batted .297, hitting five home runs and driving in 51 runs in 73 games. He was promoted to the Pittsfield, Massachusetts, team in the Double A Eastern League in 1986 and quickly began revealing his potential. He hit 12 homers and batted .306, driving in a league-leading 95 runs in 140 games; he was voted the league's most valuable player. The Cubs were impressed enough to bring him up to Chicago for the remainder of the 1986 season, where he saw limited action. He played in 22 games and hit three home runs during his brief tenure, but he was very focused and quite excited about the opportunity.

"This was everything I had been working for," he said. He made a major league salary for one month, "which was more than I had made the entire year before," he said.

From left to right: Fern Cuza (Rafael's agent); Rafael's father, José; brother, Rick; Rafael; Miguel Gallego; and brother, Andy

Palmeiro was sent back to the minors at the start of the 1987 season, playing for Iowa in the Triple A American Association, but after only 57 games, when he batted .299 and slugged 11 home runs, he was called back to Chicago. He was in the majors for good.

Palmeiro did well with the Cubs, hitting 14 homers against major league pitching and making major league money: $120,000 a year. He was now playing the outfield and first base, and in 1988 he batted .307, including a 20-game hitting streak in May. However, he hit only eight home runs and drove in only 53 runs.

He was selected to the Major League All-Star team, which toured Japan after the 1988 season, but the Cubs didn't believe he was going to be the power hitter they needed at first base and traded him to the Texas Rangers in December 1988 in an eight-player deal. To say that the

Cubs got the short end of that deal is to put it mildly. The Rangers got Palmeiro and pitchers Drew Hall and Jamie Moyer. In return, the Cubs got pitchers Paul Kilgus, Mitch Williams, and Steve Wilson, infielder Curtis Wilkerson, and two minor leaguers. Of the entire group, only Palmeiro and Moyer for the Rangers and Mitch Williams for the Cubs made any mark, and only Palmeiro and Moyer are still in the major leagues.

The Palmeiros moved to Texas and bought their first house. "I liked playing for the Rangers," Palmeiro said. "I had a lot of friends and good teammates, and the ballpark was only two minutes from my home. I was very happy there."

He started off slowly in Texas in 1989, hitting only eight home runs in his first year in the American League, but as he became accustomed to American League pitching, his numbers began to rise. He hit 14, 26, 22, and 37 home runs in his next four years with the Rangers and stepped onto the top rung of major league sluggers. In 1991 he led the American League in hits with 191 and in doubles with 49. He batted .322 and hit 26 home runs that year, earning him the honors of being named the team's most valuable player and being selected to the American League All-Star team. His runs batted in totals also kept rising steadily, and in 1993 he drove in 105 runs.

Palmeiro had a career year in 1993, his last with the Texas Rangers. He led the American League in runs scored with 124. He hit 37 home runs on a batting average of .295. But he was disappointed when the Rangers made him their salary offer for the next season of about $26 million for five years.

"It didn't seem like they cared about me one way or the other," Palmeiro said. "They just handed me this number, which they said was not negotiable, and they gave me a short amount of time to take it or leave it."

According to Rangers general manager Tom Grieve, the team was caught in the middle of a free agency decision and had to act quickly. Will Clark, Palmeiro's former teammate at Mississippi State, was also available on the free agent market after several years with the San Francisco Giants.

"We made every effort to sign Rafael," Grieve said. "He was the first choice of every person in our organization. We went after Clark only when it looked like we might end up with neither one, and we couldn't risk that. A left-handed power hitter was our number one priority."

In short, the Rangers were afraid they couldn't meet Palmeiro's price after his great year with them, and they signed Clark instead, for $30 million over five years, only slightly less than what the Orioles eventually paid Palmeiro.

In October 1993, after having completed five years in the major leagues, Palmeiro declared himself a free agent. This meant he was

open to the highest bidder, and he was well pre-
pared for the challenge of marketing his skills.

Rafael is teaching his son Patrick to play baseball.

Rafael enjoyed the years he spent with the Texas Rangers. The family bought their first house in Texas and they still maintain a home there to this day.

Says his agent, Fern Cuza, "Rafael is very sharp and he is very easy to work with. He knows the market for ball players, he's got a good head for business. We worked together to get him the best deal, and he was a great help to us in determining what the market was for him."

The best deal came from Peter Angelos and the Baltimore Orioles: $27,690,241 for five years plus bonuses, which would put the total over $30 million. There is some background to that signing.

In October 1993, Orioles manager Johnny Oates had dinner with new owner Angelos. Angelos dropped a few names the Orioles might pursue, and Oates nearly dropped his fork.

"He gave me the chills," Oates said. "I thought, 'You're kidding me.' He was talking big, expensive names."

The two most obvious free agent candidates were Will Clark and Rafael Palmeiro. Clark has had bad knees, and his power production was small compared to Palmeiro's, who was coming off a career best year. They were both 29 years old at the time, and both played first base. Palmeiro was somewhat laid back, Clark was a rah-rah guy in the dugout, but because of injuries he was almost as much on the bench as on the field. In 1984, when both were sophomores at Mississippi State, Palmeiro became the first triple crown winner (hits, home runs, runs batted in) in Southeastern Conference history. Clark was nearly as good, and it appeared the two would go one-two in the 1985 amateur draft. But suddenly things changed. Clark got added exposure as a member of the 1984 U.S. Olympic team (Cuban-born Palmeiro was not eligible). Then, as a junior, Clark won the Golden Spikes award as the nation's best collegiate player after Palmeiro went into a slump.

Palmeiro is known today as a powerful home run hitter. But the Chicago Cubs traded him away early in his career when they thought he would never become a power hitter.

Clark became the number two pick in the draft behind B.J. Surhoff, who played for the Orioles in 1995, '96, and '97, and Palmeiro was the number twenty-two choice in a draft loaded with talent. Clark signed with the San Francisco Giants for $160,000; Palmeiro got half as much from the Chicago Cubs.

Gary Nickels, then a scout for the Chicago Cubs, met with Rafael and Lynne at a Holiday Inn in Starkville, Mississippi. The deal was made in less than 24 hours, and Palmeiro was Cub property.

"The gist of it was, Rafael was anxious to get signed to prove to people he was better than the twenty-second pick in the country," Nickels said. "I remember when he signed. It was just a statement, not a boast, when he said, 'I'm going to be successful, I'm going to be a good major league player.' Rafael had the same determination and focus then that he does now. The feeling I got was this is a guy that wants to win very, very badly. He had a burning desire to achieve, to achieve in a big way. I came away thinking 'Wow!'"

In December 1993, it was the Orioles' turn to deal. After five days of intense negotiation, and while Johnny Oates rang Christmas sleigh bells in the background, the Orioles handed out the biggest free agent contract in their history.

"It would have been nice for things to work out in Texas," Palmeiro said after the signing. "But I'm an Oriole now and I'm not looking back. It's good to be going to a team that wants you. It's a team that can win."

A measure of Palmeiro's intensity can be gathered from his statement to Orioles owner Peter Angelos when they first met after Palmeiro's signing. "You'll never be sorry for signing me, Mr. Angelos. I'll break my back for you."

According to John Steadman, a sportswriter who writes a column for The [Baltimore] *Sun*, the Orioles were attracted by Palmeiro's modesty as well as his hitting, and they regarded him as an "All-American guy" who would give himself unselfishly to the Orioles.

Said shortstop Cal Ripken Jr., "The Palmeiro signing is certainly reason to get excited. We've been close the last two years and we needed to go that extra step. Raffy might be that final step, but no one is smart enough to know what is going to happen in a baseball season."

Palmeiro was careful not to cast himself as a savior, however. "I don't think one player can make the difference. I think it takes all the players and the coaching staff. We just have to have a winning attitude and we'll do all right.

"As far as leadership is concerned, I lead by example, by working hard and playing every day. I'm not a rah-rah guy, I'm not the kind of player who's going to get in people's faces. I've never been that way, but I've still had the respect of my teammates and the fans."

The return of Palmeiro to Texas for a four-game series shortly after the opening of the 1994 season was not quite as pleasant as his welcome in Baltimore, however. He went 0 for 4 in the first game, was booed by the crowd, and was knocked off the plate by a pitch.

From left to right: Roberto Alomar, Cal Ripken Jr., and Rafael posed for this picture during spring training 1996.

"The fans really surprised me with the way they booed," he said. "The five years are gone, the cord's been cut. I still have the fans in Baltimore. They'll support me no matter what."

Some of the Texas fans sort of apologized for the first-game treatment by hoisting a banner in the upper deck in right field during the second game that said: "Rafael: Thanks for the Memories." Palmeiro responded by hitting a home run that sailed over the banner in the Orioles' 6–4 victory.

Palmeiro had a good year in his first season with the Orioles, playing almost flawlessly in the field, batting .319 (fourth best in Orioles history), slugging 23 homers, and driving in 76 runs.

He stepped up the pace in 1995, with a career high 39 home runs, the third most ever by an Oriole, and 104 runs batted in. He again hit 39 home runs and batted in an astounding 142 runs in 1996, leading the Orioles into the American League playoffs. The fantasy baseball magazine produced by The Sporting News noted that Palmeiro is "a steady hitter and run-producer who seems to get better every season. Some thought he had peaked when he turned in a breakthrough season with 37 homers and 105 runs batted in for the Rangers in 1993, but he has had higher combined RBI/at-bat ratios over the past three years with Baltimore. He is also durable, having played 159 of a possible 162 games in 1996."

He won the Louis M. Hatter award as most valuable Oriole player in 1995 and 1996. The award is named after a distinguished sportswriter for The [Baltimore] *Sun* who covered the

Orioles for 27 years and was considered the Dean of American sportswriters. Mr. Hatter would have been proud of this award in his name to the self-effacing Palmeiro.

Palmeiro has also seen Orioles history being made and says the most exciting moment in his baseball career came in September 1995, when teammate Cal Ripken Jr. tied and then broke a record once thought to be untouchable. Lou Gehrig had played 2,130 consecutive games for the New York Yankees over parts of three decades, and on September 6, 1995, Ripken tied the record and passed it the next night.

Ripken had been in the Orioles' starting lineup for every game since May 30, 1982. On Thursday, September 7, President Bill Clinton attended the game to watch Ripken break the record, and Palmeiro brought his oldest son, Patrick, to meet the President. Palmeiro took off Patrick's baseball cap and handed it to the President to autograph, but Patrick reached out and said, "No, that's Mommy's hat!" Palmeiro was only slightly embarrassed.

When the game became official after the fifth inning, the crowd stood and began roaring in excitement. Cal ran off the field as the number 2,131 was unfurled, then stepped out of the dugout and waved. A few seconds later, Palmeiro was among Ripken's teammates who pushed him out of the dugout for a memorable lap around the stadium, during which he slapped and shook hands with the fans. Palmeiro thought nothing could quite equal those two days in baseball history.

More history was made in 1996. On April 30, the Orioles and the Yankees broke the major league record for the longest nine-inning game, which lasted 4 hours and 21 minutes, topping a 4:18 marathon by the Los Angeles Dodgers and San Francisco Giants in October 1962. In September, Palmeiro was there when teammate Eddie Murray hit his 500th home run, making Murray a sure shot to become a member of the Baseball Hall of Fame.

Palmeiro still has the same enthusiasm and love of baseball he had when he was a kid. He loves the sound of fans cheering, he appreciates the financial security his career provides for his wife and two children, and he likes the satisfaction he feels when he's doing well.

"It takes a lot of hard work to be a good hitter in the majors," he says. "You have to be mentally strong. You know, it's a lot of games and you face a lot of different pitchers, different styles. There are times when you're not going to feel right. That's when you need to be strong mentally and you need to stay positive in your thinking. This has helped me through the years, and I'm getting better at it.

"My approach to hitting is this: I'm going to drive the ball. I don't choke up with two strikes. It's going to cost me some points on my batting average, but as long as I'm producing for the team, that's okay."

Rafael is mobbed for autographs.

Asked by a sportswriter his thoughts on Cuban players who have been defecting to the United States to play baseball, Palmeiro said, "I'd like to see them come over here and get the same opportunity as I got. I'd like to see these guys show their talents here at this level. They live and die baseball in Cuba, and I would like to see the best players come here and show what they can do.

"I would like the two governments to work it out where Cuban players can come to the U.S. and play. Actually, I would like to see a different government down there so that all people, not just baseball players, can come and go as they please. I just don't see how it's going to happen, though."

As part of his commitment to baseball, Palmeiro follows a rigorous off-season conditioning program. He lifts weights four times a week starting in November, and he starts running in January. "I ride the bike four times a week all along, and I start hitting in January about three or four times a week."

Palmeiro sets high standards for himself, and although he knows it is impossible to be at his best every moment, he still makes this his goal. During the 1996 season, he went 16 games without an extra base hit, a first for him. It disgusted him, but he ended that streak on May 12 when he hit a pair of two-run homers against Milwaukee.

Teammate Brady Anderson was asked about Palmeiro's mood when he was not hitting well.

Son Preston is an Orioles fan, too.

"Who knows," Anderson said. "He only doesn't hit for about one week a year and then he complains about it. He's the only guy in the world who could be on a pace for thirty homers and act like he thinks he's a banjo hitter."

Says Palmeiro, "Hitting is such a weird thing. Players go through slumps, but maybe the next streak will be as good as this one was bad. I'm living off a dream right now. Reality might set in soon, but my career has taken off and I intend to enjoy it while I can."

The Palmeiro family: Rafael, wife, Lynne, Preston (left) and Patrick

Hitting is just part of Palmeiro's baseball talent. He has a lot of pride in his defensive abilities, also. "I know people don't notice my

defense," he says, "but if you look over the last three to five years, I'm up there with the best of them. In 1994, I tied in fielding percentage. I made four errors. The year before, I made three. I've gotten better and I keep working on it. My goal is to win a Gold Glove one day. I don't want to mess up a game on defense. I'd rather strike out and lose the game striking out than to make an error and lose a game."

Palmeiro has not ignored his civic responsibilities on the theory that those who are fortunate and benefit from society should give something back. He distributes about a thousand free tickets annually to youngsters from needy families. The recipients, dubbed Raffy's Rascals, sit in the right field stands where Palmeiro hits many of his home runs. He has been involved in several charitable organizations in Texas and Baltimore and has done public service announcements for various education campaigns. In fact, Palmeiro, with his dark mustache and handsome Latin features, has become familiar to Baltimore television viewers as a commercial spokesman for BGE, the area electric utility.

He has some advice to young aspiring baseball players, which he told to freelance writer Barbara Marvis: "You should work hard and stay focused. Take the sport seriously, but enjoy it, too. Once you have a goal in life, never stop trying to reach it. Don't let other people tell you what you can't do."

CHAPTER FOUR
Rafael Palmeiro and the 1996 Pennant Race
The Wackiest Season in Baseball History

T he sunny but chilly afternoon of April 2, 1996, was the start of something beautiful for the Baltimore Orioles, who hadn't been in the American League playoffs for 13 long years, or since their world championship year of 1983. Their ace pitcher, Mike Mussina, was on the mound, and behind him was a re-vamped team, including All-Star second baseman Roberto Alomar, just acquired from Toronto; shortstop Cal Ripken Jr.; slugging out-fielder–designated hitter Bobby Bonilla; the swift, homer-happy Brady Anderson in center; and, of course, Rafael Palmeiro at first base and coming off his best ever year.

The high expectations for the team were noted by Palmeiro during spring training in Florida. "This team is awesome," he told Balti-more *Sun* sportswriter John Eisenberg. "It's winning time, isn't it? There aren't many years when you can have a legitimate chance to win it all, but it's true. I've been on some great teams, but never one with talent like this. We'll win a

President Bill Clinton threw the ceremonial opening day pitch at Camden Yards, April 1996.

lot of games. It's worked out for the best for me, but I'm thinking 'we,' not 'me.' I'm in the right place, on a better team, in a city that loves baseball, with an owner that's committed to winning. We have a sense of confidence now."

The eventual short answers to all of that were Yes and No, Rafael, but springtime exuberance is a healthy part of the game of baseball, and the season turned out to be one of the strangest and most exciting seasons in recent Orioles history.

The strange part started even before the first game, when Orioles owner Peter Angelos and the President of the United States, Bill Clinton, retired to the batting cages underneath the stands at the Camden Yards stadium for some warm-up pitches. What a peculiar sight:

the owner of the Orioles warming up the leader
of the free world.

The President is known as a prideful,
deliberate person who does his homework, and
he was still agitated by his performance of a
couple of years earlier at Camden Yards when
he failed to get the ceremonial opening pitch to
the plate. Cal Ripken Jr. had needled the President on his performance. "I kidded him a little
bit about the last time he threw out the first ball
here, how he didn't go all the way to the mound
and didn't get the ball to the plate," Ripken said.
Mr. Clinton was taking no chances on a repeat.
"He must have thrown me a hundred pitches,"
Angelos said. "He was absolutely not going to
go out there and not throw the ball over the
plate."

There was no idle chatter between the
two. "He was intent on what he was doing,"
Angelos said. "He wasn't playing around."

The President then went out on the field
and threw a strike to Orioles catcher Chris
Hoiles. "But I'll bet he'll have a sore arm tomorrow," Angelos said with a laugh.

Not laughing were the Kansas City
Royals, Baltimore's opening day opponents.
Mussina pitched a strong seven innings and
Ripken drove in the first three Oriole runs in a
4–2 victory before a roaring, sellout crowd of
46,818.

The Orioles won their first four games,
and after two weeks they were 11 and 2, including a two-game sweep of the American League

champion Cleveland Indians, and the fans were talking about an easy path to the World Series in October. But the baseball season travels a long and unpredictable road, and the Orioles' orange and black colors quickly turned black and blue in the following days.

They lost six straight games after reaching the 11 and 2 mark, and the reason became apparent on April 19 when the Texas Rangers scored 16 runs in the eighth inning of a game in Texas before winning 26–7. Orioles pitching had collapsed. The staff's earned run average had soared to 5.01 from 2.55. Orioles pitchers couldn't get anybody out.

By April 23, they had played themselves back in the pack of the American League East. During their losing streak they were scoring an average of six runs a game and still losing, despite manager Davey Johnson's every effort to stimulate the pitching staff by moving pitchers in and out of the starting rotation.

There were other diversions. Bobby Bonilla was made the designated hitter and didn't like it. He wanted to play right field, and he said sitting on the bench was damaging his batting average. "I just don't feel part of the game," he said.

Johnson finally gave in at the end of April, when Bonilla's average had dropped to .211. Bonilla went to the outfield for good. The move turned around his season, and by the end he had hit 28 home runs and driven in 116 on a .287 batting average.

There was another diversion. The Orioles began thinking about moving Cal Ripken to third base and starting Manny Alexander at shortstop. They felt that Ripken, at the age of 35, couldn't quite do it anymore in the field, but the proposal created such controversy that the experiment wasn't tried until July. Alexander didn't perform well at bat or in the field, perhaps because of the pressure of following an icon, and the experiment lasted only six games.

There was another strange event on April 30, when the Orioles and the Yankees locked up at Camden Yards in the longest nine-inning game ever played in the major leagues to that date. It lasted 4 hours and 21 minutes. The longer it went, the uglier it got. And the uglier it got, the longer it lasted.

The Yankees won, 13–10, but only the most patient of fans from the original crowd of 43,117 at Camden Yards remained when the game finally ended at 11:57 P.M., Eastern Standard Time, after Yankee first baseman Tino Martinez hit a three-run homer.

There were 400 pitches, eight pitching changes, four lead changes, two ejections, and innumerable mound conferences. A total of 96 baseballs were used, probably also a record, but who knows? The previous longevity record had been 4:18 in a game between the Los Angeles Dodgers and San Francisco Giants on October 2, 1962.

To make the game even stranger, Davey Johnson did something no Orioles manager had ever done: he pulled Ripken from the lineup and inserted Alexander as a pinch runner. Alexander was immediately picked off first base while the fans groaned and Ripken stewed in the dugout. Johnson wondered what the fuss was about. "I was just trying to win the game," he said.

Palmeiro was asked afterward if the game felt that long. "It felt like two days and twenty-one minutes," he said. Only two weeks before, the Orioles and Rangers had played for 4 hours and 15 minutes; the Orioles lost 26–7.

To make matters worse for the Orioles, Palmeiro was in an unaccustomed 3-for-28 slump. By May 12, he had gone 16 games without an extra base hit, and all he could say was "Wow! I've never done this before."

It was evident he was frustrated. He threw his bat after making an out on May 10, then slammed his helmet to the ground with both hands after lining out with the bases loaded the next night.

He was on a 32-homer, 117-RBI pace even during the slump, which says something about his high standards.

"I've thought about it a lot," he said of the slump. "It's a combination of things. They're pitching around me a little bit, and I'm missing my pitch too much, which runs the count up. I've been fouling off pitches I should have hit well, or swinging and missing. When I'm on my game, I'm not going to work the pitch count. You give me a pitch I can handle, I'm not going to miss it."

"Hitting is such a weird thing," he said. "Players go through slumps and you don't understand why it happens. Maybe the next streak will be as good as this one was bad."

The words were hardly out of his mouth when, on May 12, he hit a pair of two-run homers against Milwaukee, including the 200th of his career. He was on his way, never to look back.

Palmeiro was 10 for 22 in the next five games, including three home runs and 14 runs batted in. During a game against the Brewers, he went 5 for 6 and drove in six runs, and his batting average moved from an anemic .248 to a respectable .278.

"I just kept working hard trying to fine-tune my swing and get comfortable," he said. "It was mental. It's part of the game. Now I feel like I'm back."

Nonetheless, the Orioles were 8 and 15 since their 11 and 2 start, and the pitching was striving just to stay alive, much less win, by the middle of May. Their problems would remain well past the annual All-Star game in the second week of July, despite Palmeiro's heroics at bat and a resurgence by Cal Ripken, who included among his heroics a three-homer, eight-RBI game on May 28.

By June 10, Palmeiro was batting .324, with 13 home runs and 52 runs batted in, but it was becoming apparent that he would not make the American League All-Star team. The votes were coming in, and he wasn't among the top eight first basemen, a circumstance that irked

Palmeiro, his teammates, and Orioles fans. Palmeiro was playing a position loaded with heavy hitters like Mo Vaughn of Boston, Frank Thomas of the Chicago White Sox, and Mark McGwire of Oakland. Even his former teammate, Will Clark of Texas, whose numbers were far less than Palmeiro's, was ahead of him.

It has been a rite of summer for him to put up big numbers but watch the All-Star game on TV. Frustrated, he called the voting procedure "bogus," but said that he would keep "doing my job. If I go, fine. If not, I'll take my days off."

To emphasize his point, Palmeiro went 4 for 5 the same day the first All-Star voting numbers came out, drove in three runs, and scored three runs. He hit safely in 19 of the last 23 games, with a .433 average in that stretch.

But Vaughn and Thomas were also putting up monster numbers, leading or near the lead in homers, batting averages, and runs batted in. "I can name the two guys right now who should go—Mo Vaughn and Frank Thomas," Palmeiro said.

The Orioles pitching staff was still getting hammered, however, and the team finally ended a three-game losing streak on June 28 when they beat the Yankees in New York, 7–4. Once again it was Palmeiro leading the way. He hit two two-run homers, his nineteenth and twentieth of the season. "It gets us back to four and a half games behind the Yankees," Palmeiro said. "I feel like we're going to get going."

The All-Star frustration surfaced again just before the All-Star break in July. Palmeiro *Rafael hits another home run!*

didn't make the team, but he did hit a home run and drive in four against the Toronto Blue Jays on July 2, giving him a total of 76 runs batted in, second in the league, with half the season to be played.

Palmeiro's expression never changed when reporters read him the list of players who were picked. He didn't bang a chair or pound a fist. There were no angry words. In fact, he cracked a joke about changing his position. "I'm going to play second base next year," he said, laughing.

Manager Johnson called Palmeiro into his office, offered him condolences and left him with this, according to an account in the Baltimore *Sun* by sportswriter Buster Olney: Let's win the World Series, and then next year, when Johnson would manage the All-Star team, he would pick Palmeiro "even if he was hitting .250."

Since the All-Star break of 1995, Palmeiro had been unstoppable. He had batted .321, with 45 homers and 133 RBI's, and he was still going strong.

Then came the All-Star game in Philadelphia on July 9 and another strange twist to the Orioles season. Cal Ripken had dodged inside pitches and hurdled oncoming runners for 14 seasons, avoiding serious injury long enough to become the Iron Man of Baseball. So imagine the reaction when he was nearly knocked out of the American League lineup by the freakiest of freak accidents.

The team was standing for photos to be taken before the All-Star game when White Sox pitcher Roberto Hernandez lost his balance on the platform and whacked Ripken squarely in the face with his elbow while trying to regain his balance. The blow broke Ripken's nose and jeopardized his 2,239-game playing streak.

Ripken held his nose for a second in shock, then headed for the American League

In the freakiest of accidents, Cal Ripken broke his nose before the All-Star game in 1996.

locker room as blood ran down his face. He emerged a few minutes later with his nose packed and straightened, ready to make his thirteenth straight All-Star start at shortstop.

"It was a freak thing," Ripken said, as the embarrassed Hernandez stood by. "Can't blame anybody for that."

Said Hernandez: "It was bleeding pretty bad. I offered him my shirt to help stop the bleeding. I thought for a while I was going to need a bodyguard the next time I came to Baltimore. If this ends the streak, I'm dead."

Said Ripken: "I didn't want to go down in All-Star history as the only player to be injured during a team picture."

Anticipation among Orioles fans ran high immediately after the All-Star break. The hated Yankees were coming to town for a four-game series, the biggest of the year, and capacity crowds were at Camden Yards to see their team beat up their fearsome rivals. The Orioles were only four games behind New York, which had taken the Eastern Division lead from the Orioles on April 30 and had held it ever since.

But Orioles bats went into hibernation for a midsummer nap. The Orioles lost the first game 3–2 when the Yankees scored two runs in the ninth inning. The next game was rained out, and on July 13, the two teams met for a climactic doubleheader. The Orioles lost the opener 7–5 when Darryl Strawberry smashed a two-run homer, then fell dead, 4–1, to Yankee pitching ace Andy Pettitte in the nightcap. The last game of the series was equally as disheartening when the Orioles lost in the tenth inning, 3–2. (The Yankees eventually won the regular season series 10–3).

So they were continuing their uneven ways after the All-Star break despite the fact that of the next 22 games, 18 would be played at home. They lost 15 of the 22, including 13 at home. The Minnesota Twins swept them in three straight and they lost three of four to Cleveland. The Yankee sweep seemed to have taken the heart out of them. Orioles fans began counting them out of the American League race.

So did some in the Orioles management. On July 28, with the Orioles below .500 at 51 and 52, manager Johnson and general manager Pat Gillick sat down to talk about the future. Should the team write off the season and trade Bonilla and David Wells, their best pitcher over the previous six weeks? Should they step back, in the words of Johnson, by trading some veterans for good, young players, so they could step forward in 1997? Do they tell 28,000 season ticket holders that they've given up on this $48 million team and are going to prepare for the future?

There was strong sentiment in the organization for trading the veterans, but a wiser head prevailed. Owner Angelos stepped in and said, in so many words, "Not on your life!"

The Orioles would not trade, they would not give up, they would come back. With two months still to play and only five games be-

Orioles Manager Davey Johnson, right, argues for his team. In fact, Johnson has been ejected from several games for arguing unfair calls.

hind Seattle for the wild card spot in the American League East, they would keep their lineup intact.

Angelos proved to be right. Three weeks later, the Orioles were back in the thick of it, and Palmeiro was leading the charge.

On August 16, Palmeiro drove in six runs to lead the Orioles to a 14–3 victory over the Oakland Athletics in the first game of a doubleheader, then hit two run-scoring doubles in the second game to bring his team a 5–4 victory. The Orioles ran their winning streak to five games and moved to within five and a half games of the league-leading Yankees and just one game behind the Chicago White Sox for a wild card spot. They were serving notice that they were no longer the under-achieving team that had stumbled through the early summer with little sense of direction except down.

"I don't know what it is," Palmeiro said. "We've got a great hitting team. Sometimes it takes a few at-bats to get going." With more than six weeks remaining, he had 111 runs batted in and was on a pace to drive in 148 runs. He also had 30 home runs.

"He does it so easy," Johnson said. "He has such a sweet, sweet swing."

By August 20, the Orioles were back in the race after winning 14 of 20 games, most of them on the road. "A lot of things that didn't happen early have come late," said Johnson. The Orioles had traded pitcher Kent Mercker for first baseman–designated hitter Eddie Murray on July 21, and his big bat was helping the offense. Murray, a long-time favorite of Orioles fans, had come out of the Orioles farm system in the early 1980s and later played for the Los Angeles Dodgers and Cleveland Indians. At the age of 40, his career was fading, but he could still hit the long ball.

On September 4, the Orioles walloped five homers against the California Angels and took the major league lead in homers with 221, moving to within 18 homers of the all-time record of 241 set by the New York Yankees in 1961. (The Orioles easily broke the record, with 257 home runs). The Yankee lineup in 1961 had included Mickey Mantle, who hit 54 home runs, and Roger Maris, who hit 61 homers.

The Orioles offense was erratic, having been shut out seven times, but since the All-Star break they had hit 88 homers in 53 games, an incredible rate of 1.66 homers per game.

One of the remarkable stories of the Orioles' 1996 season was the performance of center fielder Brady Anderson, who had hit an amazing 43 home runs by September 3. He finished with 50 home runs, and the left-handed batter was as surprised as anyone with his power surge. His previous career high had been 21 homers.

Power hitter Brady Anderson hit a whopping 50 home runs in the 1996 season.

The tension of the stretch run was beginning to tell on many of the teams in the league. Texas manager Johnny Oates locked himself in his office and refused to talk to anyone after the Rangers fumbled away a game to Minnesota. And Lou Piniella, manager of the Seattle Mariners, lost his cool and threatened the under-achieving members of his pitching staff with unemployment after the Mariners' bullpen nearly blew a seven-run lead in the ninth inning against the Boston Red Sox. The Orioles and Yankees were only four games apart for the American League East title with three weeks to play.

Then came another historic moment for the Orioles. On September 6, the first anniversary of Cal Ripken's historic breaking of Lou Gehrig's consecutive game streak, Eddie Murray hit his 500th home run and became only the third player in major league history to reach 500 homers and 3,000 hits.

Murray turned Camden Yards into a rapturous carnival scene when he hit a first-pitch fastball into the right field bleachers off Detroit Tigers pitcher Felipe Lira in the seventh inning to end the suspense that had been building since he hit his 499th homer at the Kingdome in Seattle three days earlier. Only Willie Mays and Hank Aaron, either of whom it could be argued was the best player ever, had reached both of baseball's most revered offensive plateaus.

Eddie Murray hit his 500th career home run on September 6, 1996. He became only the third player in major league history to reach 500 homers and 3,000 hits.

"Only the third guy to do that?" Murray said. "It's still hard to see yourself mentioned in that same company."

Baltimore businessman Michael Lasky later bought Murray's home run ball for $300,000 from the fan who caught it and gave it to the Babe Ruth Museum in Baltimore, where it is on display.

Another record was about to fall, that of 6-foot-4 Diamond Jim Gentile, who had played first base for the Orioles in the early 1960s. On September 23, Palmeiro drove in his 140th run, leaving him just one run short of tying Gentile's all-time Orioles record of runs batted in set in 1961.

"More power to him," said Gentile from his home in Edmond, Oklahoma. At 62, he is retired from an insurance career, but he still participates in various major league fantasy camps around the country. "It's great to be in the record books all these years. Records are made to be broken. This one lasted thirty-five years."

Until Palmeiro's total rose into the 130s, no one had seriously threatened Gentile's record. Outfielder Frank Robinson never drove in more than 122, and first baseman Boog Powell's peak was 121, which shows how powerful Palmeiro's performance was.

"I understand Palmeiro's a great guy, and obviously a great hitter," Gentile said. "I hope he goes on to drive in many more runs."

The key for Palmeiro, as it was for Gentile, is that there were a lot of good hitters in the club who obligingly got on base frequently. Just as Palmeiro had Roberto Alomar, Bobby Bonilla, Cal Ripken, and Eddie Murray, Gentile had Brooks Robinson, Russ Snyder, Jackie Brandt, and Whitey Herzog.

Gentile's big season was peppered with highlights. He collected nine RBI's in a game in Minnesota in which he became the first player in major league history to smash two grand slams in succession. Gentile got 20 of his runs batted in on grand slams, hitting five to set an American League single season record and tying Ernie Banks of the Chicago Cubs for the major league record.

Palmeiro's performance was bringing him national attention after years of having his statistical performance overlooked. By September 11, he was third in the league in RBI's, sixth in total bases and eighth with the number of multi-hit games. He was tied for fifth with 75 extra-base hits.

"I think if you look at his numbers in the 1990s and compare them to anyone else, he's as good as anybody," Johnson said. "You have to be on teams that win to really get national recognition. If the Orioles win a couple of pennants, he'll probably get the most valuable player award if he keeps up those numbers." Before the 1996 season, Palmeiro's teams had a combined winning percentage of .497, beginning with the 1986 Chicago Cubs.

"It's exciting," Palmeiro said. "I look forward to coming to the ballpark."

The race for the Eastern Division playoffs also was exciting, but all the contenders were staggering down the stretch. Orioles pitching, which had recovered somewhat from its early season letdown, was coming apart again with a little more than a week to go in the season. By September 24, after winning 31 of 46 games, they lost two in a row and five of the previous eight. They weren't going to catch the Yankees, who also had pitching problems, but they were hanging on.

Seattle and Chicago, which along with Baltimore were contenders for a wild card playoff spot, were also burdened with pitching problems, and the Orioles held a one-and-a-half-game lead over Seattle.

On September 26, Palmeiro broke Jim Gentile's Oriole RBI record by hitting a two-run homer in a 6–2 victory over the Boston Red Sox, giving him 142 for the year. But the next day there occurred one of those unaccountable incidents that nearly derailed the Orioles' run for the playoffs. Their normally laid-back All-Star second baseman, Roberto Alomar, spat in umpire John Hirschbeck's face in a rage over a called third strike and risked suspension for the remainder of the season. It was the first inning of a game in Toronto. Angry at the call, Alomar began yelling at the umpire as he returned to the dugout. Hirschbeck warned Alomar several times to quit complaining, and when Alomar shouted, "Pay attention to the game," Hirschbeck ejected him from the game. Alomar ran from the dugout to confront the umpire. Davey Johnson tried to wedge himself between Alomar and Hirschbeck, but Alomar jerked his head forward and, television replays showed, clearly spat in the umpire's face.

Alomar acknowledged the spitting. "I'm not going to lie," he said. "He called me a name and I called him the same name back. They can do anything to you, but you can't do anything back. I've never seen anyone miss a pitch so far outside." Alomar said he "used to respect" Hirschbeck, but suggested that the umpire had changed since he lost a young son, John, in 1993 to a rare disease called adrenaluko dystrophy. Another son also has the disease.

Umpire John Hirschbeck (left), Robbie Alomar (center), and Davey Johnson (right) argue over Hirschbeck's bad call.

"I know that's something real tough in life for a person," Alomar said. "He just got bitter."

Said Hirschbeck: "Twenty-one years I've been umpiring, and never before . . ."

A suspension for Alomar in the waning days of the season would have been fatal to the

Orioles. To make matters worse, the Orioles lost the game 3–2, but they clinched a tie for the playoff spot when Seattle lost to Oakland that same night.

The Orioles needed one more victory, and that transpired the very next night when, ironically, shortly after it was learned that Alomar would be suspended for five regular season games, Alomar hit a home run in the tenth inning to give the Orioles a 3–2 victory over Toronto. Alomar appealed the sentence, and the suspension would not start until the beginning of the 1997 season. The Umpires Association vigorously opposed the penalty, saying it was too lenient and should begin immediately, but it was overruled. Good thing for the Orioles: Alomar was a vital part of the lineup.

Alomar, his good-guy image tarnished, eventually apologized to Hirschbeck and contributed $50,000 toward research into the rare brain disease that had killed Hirschbeck's son. For his part, Hirschbeck said, "What happened last year happened, and it's over. For anyone to think I would hold any animosity toward him is ridiculous."

The long up-and-down ordeal was over. The Orioles would face the powerful Cleveland Indians, who had clinched the Central Division championship on September 17, in a best-of-five game series. It was Baltimore's first playoff series in 13 years.

In the interlude, the Orioles and their fans could reflect on some offbeat statistics from the regular season, including Brady Anderson's record-setting 50 home runs and the Orioles' major league home-run record of 257.

Cal Ripken set an American League record for most double plays participated in by a shortstop in his career—1,565. The major league record was 1,590, held by Ozzie Smith of the St. Louis Cardinals. With Smith nearing retirement, Ripken was expected to overtake him in 1997.

Roberto Alomar hit homers from both sides of the plate in two games. That tied an American League record.

Ripken extended his major league record for career homers by a shortstop, 345. He also set a major league record for most years leading in games played.

Eddie Murray, aside from hitting his 500th home run, extended his major league record for games played at first base, 2,413, and most assists for a first baseman, 1,865.

On the sad side, the Orioles tied an American League record by winning only one complete game shutout, that by Mike Mussina on September 7.

It was Anderson who fired the first shot in the opening game of a best-of-five series against Cleveland at Camden Yards on October 1, and he used his best weapon, the home run. He bashed a high, fat curveball from Cleveland pitcher Charles Nagy far over the right field wall as the first Oriole batter in the first inning, and the Orioles never looked back. They hit four homers, including a grand slam by Bobby Bonilla, and Palmeiro batted in a run with a double as the Orioles won 10–4.

The next day they pushed the Indians to the edge of extinction with a 7–4 victory, led once again by Brady Anderson, who hit his second homer in two days to help the Orioles to a 4–0 lead in the fifth inning. The Indians came back to tie it 4–4, but Ripken smacked a clutch double in the eighth to set up the winning rally.

The teams moved to Cleveland for game three on October 4, and the Indians lived to play another day by winning, 9–4, on the strength of Albert Belle's grand slam home run that shattered a 4–4 tie in the seventh inning. But the Indians were living on borrowed time.

Game four was the strangest of all. Palmeiro put the Orioles in front with a 375-foot home run into the right field stands in the second inning, and Bonilla immediately followed with another. The television announcer said he thought Nagy, pitching again for Cleveland on three days' rest, "got a little tentative" after Palmeiro's homer, and this helped Bonilla.

The Indians tied the game at 2–2 in the fourth, then went ahead 3–2 in the next inning. Meanwhile, Orioles batters were swinging at air, striking out at an embarrassing pace as Nagy moved easily through their lineup. The Orioles were also committing errors and generally playing as though they were really tired of the whole thing. Their strikeouts eventually totaled an astounding 23, a playoff record.

But Alomar brought them back. With two strikes on him and two out in the ninth, he lined a single to left to drive in the tying run, then struck a dramatic home run over the right center field fence in the twelfth inning against Cleveland reliever José Mesa to give the Orioles a wild, champagne-soaked ending to the series.

Unfortunately, and through a peculiar set of circumstances, it was their last big hurrah. The mighty Yankees, who had easily beaten the Texas Rangers in their best-of-five series, three games to one, would play the Orioles for the American League championship.

Game one of the best-of-seven series began in Yankee Stadium on October 10, and it was the strangest of all the strange games the Orioles played in 1996.

It started off innocently and favorably enough, with Brady Anderson and Rafael Palmeiro doing their thing early in the game. Anderson homered in the third inning and Palmeiro in the fourth off the Yankees' 21-game winner, Andy Pettitte, to give the Orioles a 3–2 lead. The Orioles pushed across another run in the sixth to make it 4–2, but the Yankees got another run in the seventh to cut the Oriole lead to one run.

Then came the strange eighth inning. With one out, Yankee shortstop Derek Jeter struck a towering fly ball that Oriole right fielder Tony Tarasco appeared to have in his sights. He backed up to the right field wall and raised his glove to make the catch. Then zoop! The ball disappeared liked magic. Tarasco stood there empty-handed, a puzzled look on his face, as umpire Rich Garcia signaled a home run for Jeter. A hand belonging to 12-year-old Jeff Maier had flashed out from the seats above Tarasco and deflected the ball into the stands.

While Orioles players ran screaming onto the field to protest the call and exuberant Yankee fans gave the youngster high fives, Jeter circled the bases with the tying run.

"I just leaned over and it jumped into my glove," the baby-faced Orioles killer said to a group of reporters and TV cameramen, who had quickly surrounded him in the stands. "I didn't mean to do anything wrong. It just happened. I'm a Yankee fan, but I didn't mean to do anything to change the outcome of the game or do anything bad to the Orioles."

The ball had popped out of Jeff's glove and was lost to the throng of fans nearby, but he became an instant celebrity nonetheless. He appeared on several TV programs, including *The Today Show*, and was headed for more attention when his father called a halt.

"This is too much," his father said. "We don't want any money. We just want him to lead a normal kid's life."

The fan interference rule says that any batted or thrown ball is immediately dead when a fan touches it, and the umpire shall impose such penalties as in his opinion will nullify the act of interference. Umpire Garcia could have called Jeter out, which probably would have

Jeff Maier, New York Yankee fan, shows where the ball went.

started a riot in Yankee Stadium, or he could have given him a ground rule double if he thought the ball had been going to hit the wall.

Instant replay clearly showed that Jeff was leaning over the playing field when he touched the ball and knocked it into the stands for a home run. Umpire Garcia said he didn't see Jeff reach out and touch the ball, and he wasn't going to change his decision. Instant replays are not considered in baseball, as they used to be in pro football.

Davey Johnson and several Orioles players argued the call for ten minutes, and Johnson was thrown out of the game, but nothing changed, and the game went into extra innings.

Yankee center fielder Bernie Williams settled the matter leading off the eleventh inning. When Oriole reliever Randy Myers threw him a high slider, Williams smacked it over the left field wall for a 5–4 Yankee victory.

However, the Orioles were not rattled by their weird loss. Led by Palmeiro, who in game one had gone 3 for 3, scored three times, and drove in a run with his homer, and pitcher David Wells, they came back to win game two the next day. Wells pitched six and two thirds innings of strong baseball, and Palmeiro hit a beauty of a two-run homer in the seventh inning off Yankee reliever Jeff Nelson. It soared into the areaway between the grandstand and the bleachers in Yankee Stadium to break a 2–2 tie.

Television announcer Bob Costas was moved to say this about Palmeiro: "Raffy is such a quiet hero that he's overlooked. He shouldn't be, and neither should that sweet swing, the best in baseball."

Alomar also played a large role, despite unrelenting boos from the crowd and thrown items that pelted the field. He scored a run and drove in a run with a sacrifice fly in the Orioles' 5–3 victory.

The Orioles returned to Camden Yards for game three with high hopes that they could finish off the Yankees at home—with good reason. They had Mike Mussina, their best pitcher, and a jubilant capacity crowd of 48,635 on their side. Third baseman Todd Zeile seemed to set the tone when he slugged a two-run homer in the first inning.

Mussina hadn't beaten the Yankees since May 26, 1993, but he pitched masterfully into the eighth inning while protecting a 2–1 Oriole lead. The Yankees were at bat with two outs and no one on base when the game began to come apart for Mussina and the Orioles. Mussina wouldn't retire another batter.

Mussina threw a fastball away to Derek Jeter, and the Yankee shortstop slashed it into the right field corner for a double. Mussina next threw a hanging curve to Bernie Williams, who slapped it to left field for a single, scoring Jeter. The score was tied, 2–2.

Then came a bizarre play so typical of the Orioles season. First baseman Tino Martinez hit a Mussina fastball into the left field corner for a single. Oriole left fielder B.J. Surhoff cut the ball off before it got to the wall and threw toward home to keep Williams from scoring from second. Williams, however, had stopped at third. Zeile cut off Surhoff's throw, then whirled to throw to second base to get Martinez, speeding down the base path from first base.

Realizing he had no shot at Martinez, Zeile stopped his throwing motion and the ball squirted out of his hand toward shortstop. Williams broke from third and scored easily, and the Yankees were ahead 3–2.

Designated hitter Cecil Fielder then finished Mussina off by walloping a two-run homer over the left field wall to make it 5–2 Yankees, and that's the way game three ended. The Yankees had come from behind in all five of their playoff victories, three times against the Texas Rangers and twice against the Orioles.

The Yankees pushed the Orioles to the brink of extinction in game five with an 8–4 victory sparked by the Orioles' favorite weapon, the home run. The Yankees hit four, two by Darryl Strawberry. Palmeiro showed his frustration after hitting a 400-foot fly ball caught by Bernie Williams at the base of the wall in center field in the fourth inning. He jumped up and down, shaking his fists in anger as the ball settled into Williams' glove. A lip reader would suggest he said the word damn. He did drive in a run in the second inning with a sacrifice fly.

The Orioles could now mourn lost opportunities and consider the fact that they were one game away from elimination. Only four times in postseason history had a team come back from being down three games to one to win the final three games.

An unlikely villain surfaced in game six to end the Orioles season on an ugly note. Jim Leyritz hit a home run off Oriole starter Scott Erickson to lead off the third inning. Jeter singled with one out, then Yankee third baseman Wade Boggs tapped a ground ball toward the pitching mound. Erickson reached down for it for what would have been an easy out, but he missed the ball. Williams then hit another easy ground ball toward second that could have been a double play. Alomar went down for it, and the ball went right through his legs. Jeter scored and Boggs went to third. "That ball tricked me," Alomar said. "I thought it was going to take a hop, but it stayed down." It was a rookie mistake.

With two on and two out, up came Cecil Fielder again. Erickson threw him a fastball up and in, and Fielder hit it up and out for a three-run homer and a 5–0 Yankee lead. Strawberry followed with a tremendous home run into the Yankee bullpen in left center field to make it 6–0. Five of the runs were unearned because of Alomar's error.

He's safe!

The Orioles battled back on homers by Zeile, Murray, and Bonilla, but it was too late and the Orioles lost 6–4. Rich Garcia, the same umpire who had ruled on a controversial home run by Jeter in the first game, called the final out at first base on a futile headfirst slide by Cal Ripken after a ground ball to shortstop Jeter.

The TV camera panned the Orioles dugout as the last out was made, and there was Palmeiro, head in hands, sitting forlornly on the Orioles bench.

That the Yankees went on to defeat the Atlanta Braves in the World Series four games to three after being down two games to none was of little interest to the Orioles.

CHAPTER FIVE
The 1997 Season
A Bid for the World Series

With one smooth stroke of the bat, Tony Fernandez turned the 1997 American League Championship Series into a Greek tragedy. Baltimore died.

While the Cleveland second baseman circled the bases clapping his hands in the top of the eleventh inning of the sixth game, Oriole fans knew in their hearts the season was over. Oriole bats were dead, and three outs later their feelings were confirmed. The Indians, who lost to Baltimore in the 1996 East Division series, won the game, 1–0, and the series, 4 games to 2.

Wasted was a magnificent effort by Mike Mussina, who gave up only four runs in 29 post season innings and set a post season record by striking out 15 batters in game three, a contest the Orioles lost, 2 to 1, when Marquis Grissom stole home on a suicide squeeze play that provided one of the most controversial moments of the series.

Actually, Mussina's effort in the final game was even better than the one in game three.

When the Orioles took the field at Camden Yards on October 14 trailing the Indians in the series, 3 to 1, there was no tomorrow if they didn't win. They needed a great performance from Mussina, and they got it. He pitched one-hit ball for eight innings while the Orioles rattled Charles Nagy, the Indians starter, for nine hits.

Palmeiro summed up Oriole feelings after the game. "It's going to be hard to forget this one," he said. "Last year we got beat by the Yankees. This year, we gave it away. This is hard to swallow."

His assessment was correct. The Orioles made mistakes at crucial moments, and the usually dependable bullpen let the team down. The Orioles beat the Indians in the first game on great pitching by Scott Erickson, who combined with Randy Myers to shut out the Indians, 3–0, in Cleveland. They lost the second game, 5–4, to a dramatic three-run homer by Marquis Grissom in the eighth inning, and the third game, 2–1, in 12 innings despite Mussina's great pitching.

In that game, the controversial play was a suicide squeeze with Grissom on third and running with the pitch. The batter bunted at it and the ball went off Oriole catcher Lenny Webster's glove while Grissom scored the winning run. Webster claimed that the batter had tipped the ball, but the umpire ruled otherwise, the game was over, and the Orioles trailed the series, 2 to 1.

The fourth game was the real crusher. The Orioles led at one point, 5–2, but allowed two runners to score on a wild pitch in the fifth inning. They lost on a single by Cleveland catcher Sandy Alomar in the ninth. The Orioles won the fifth game, 4–2, before the end came suddenly in the sixth game of the series.

Despite this final failure, the Orioles had many things to look back on with pleasure. They had a tremendous season. They led the American League East Division from the first day of the season to the last, only the third American League team to do so.

The Orioles defeated the powerful Seattle Mariners, the West Division champions, in the best-of-five post season series. They led the American League in attendance for the third straight year, with more than 3.7 million fans cramming the Camden Yards stadium. They overcame numerous injuries and disabilities, including a cancer operation that sidelined outfielder Eric Davis for three months, to win 98 games. They marched into Atlanta and swept the National League champion Atlanta Braves in three games, a highlight of the season.

Palmeiro again led the Orioles in home runs with 38 and runs batted in with 110, although his batting average slipped to .254, far under his normal production. His excellence in the field continued, and he won his first Gold Glove award, an honor he had sought in his entire career.

He became the first hitter in Oriole history to hit 30 or more home runs in three straight seasons. (He had 39 in 1995 and 39 again in 1996.) He also joined Boog Powell as the only Orioles to have three seasons with 35 homers or more.

The Orioles fought hard to bring the American League championship to Baltimore. But they just couldn't make it happen.

There was, however, a different mood in the Orioles' clubhouse in 1997 as they cleared out their lockers. In 1996, immediately after the Orioles were eliminated from the ALCS in five games by the New York Yankees, general manager Pat Gillick talked about tearing apart a team that depended too heavily on the long ball. This year, no one was planning to rearrange the team. "In my heart I feel we're the best team," said assistant general manager Kevin Malone. Though the Orioles fell short of their ultimate goal of reaching the World Series, their disappointment couldn't detract from their stellar performance throughout the year. They did, after all, claim their first division flag since 1983.

Rafael: Personal Tidbits

Rafael still has the same enthusiasm and love of baseball he had when he was a kid. He loves to hear the fans cheering, but most of all, he enjoys the satisfaction he gets when he is doing well. Rafael has very high standards for himself, sometimes even higher than his managers. Though he knows it is impossible to be his best at every moment, he still makes this his goal. When he is off his game, he gets disgusted with himself. During his double-A days with the Cubs, after a bad game, Rafael was known to soak his cap in mud and wear it. Though he no longer follows such rituals, he still is very disappointed when he does not do well. Once, he even went home to his wife and told her he had forgotten how to swing!

In 1996, Palmeiro felt his sense of accomplishment vanish as soon as Baltimore lost to the New York Yankees in the American League championship series. "When the season ends that way, you can't help but feel incomplete," Rafael said. "I couldn't be satisfied with how I did [in 1996] because obviously it wasn't good enough." Though *Baseball America* named him the league's second-best defensive first baseman behind J. T. Snow, Rafael was motivated to work harder in 1997. His ultimate goal has always been to win the World Series.

Though Rafael is a top player in the major leagues, he has not always received the

Patrick practices his swing

acclaim he deserves. The Baltimore announcers and fans love him, but much of the attention he receives stops there. "To me, he's never gotten the respect he deserves," said Orioles second baseman Roberto Alomar. "But baseball people know what Raffy does for our team." In 1997, Palmeiro became the first player in Orioles history to hit more than 30 home runs in three consecutive seasons! In the 1990s, only three players have more hits than he has and only four players have scored more runs. Only Cal Ripken, baseball's iron man, has played in more games. If he were part of a team that consistently went to the playoffs and/or the World Series, he might develop more star quality. He should have more of the spotlight. Time will tell. The Baltimore team has remade itself into a winner, and Rafael should soon see some of those rewards. Unlike some earlier periods in his career, he knows he is appreciated and he is finally at home with the Baltimore Orioles.

In the off-season, Rafael works out every day to stay in shape. At 6'0", weighing around

The Palmeiros welcome newborn son Preston, January 1995.

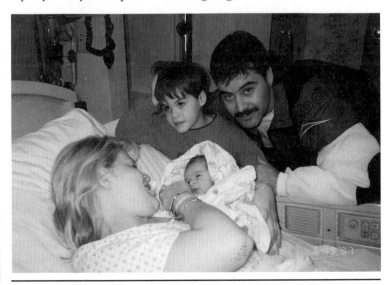

188 pounds, he lifts weights four times a week, rides a bicycle, jogs, and practices his hitting. Rafael bats and throws left. Aside from baseball, his first love is spending time with his family. Rafael, his wife, Lynne, and sons Patrick and Preston have homes in both Texas and Baltimore, Maryland. When Rafael played for the Texas Rangers, the family built a home nearby. When Rafael went to play for the Orioles, he built another home in Maryland where the family comes to live after the end of the school year. The family owns horses, which they like to ride, Rafael plays some golf now and then, and he

Preston loves to wear his Orioles uniform.

Rafael and Dad

enjoys taking the family to the movies. Because he travels so much during the baseball season, he prefers spending time at home when he is not playing ball. He would love to see his sons play baseball and he teaches them everything he knows. Patrick loves to wear his Orioles outfit and he is getting good at his swing. Preston carries a baseball all around the yard and swings his bat like a golf club.

Among the more private, lesser known facts about Palmeiro: he has a half-brother, José Jr. whom the family had to leave in Cuba when they fled in 1971. Because José was at the age of military service, he could not obtain the necessary papers in time to leave with the rest of the family. Though the family tried for many years, they could not bring José to the United States. "My friends often ask me why I ride around the streets of Havana on an old bicycle when my brother is making $6 million [playing ball for the Baltimore Orioles,]" said José. There are some things that money can't buy.

Though José had a chance to emigrate to the United States in 1992 when he came to visit the family and see Rafael play at Yankee Stadium, it would have meant leaving his wife and children behind. "You get separated and you don't know when you are going to see each other again," José said. He just couldn't do it.

In 1995, Rafael petitioned the U.S. Immigration and Naturalization Service to allow José, his wife and two children to join the rest of the family. The petition was approved, but José had to wait his turn. Rafael tried harder. He and agent Fernando Cuza traveled to Washington to present their case on Capitol Hill. When President Clinton visited Baltimore for the cel-

Rafael with his mother and brothers. From left to right: Rick, Rafael's mother, Maria, Rafael, and Andy

ebrations during Cal Ripken's historic game, Rafael spoke to him about José and handed him a letter explaining José's position. "He put it in his coat pocket," said Rafael. "He said he was going to read it that night."

Meanwhile, José was getting impatient waiting in Cuba. He is a photographer who earns a living taking pictures of weddings and parties. But economic times are hard in Cuba, and José found his means to making a living getting tougher every year.

Finally, in June 1996, Rafael received word that José and his family could come to the United States. He is now reunited with the rest of the family in Miami, where Rafael bought his brother a home.

After all the grief that Fidel Castro has brought to the Palmeiro family, this was only one more chapter. The family is angry that Castro continues to rule Cuba and they have vowed never to return. In April 1997, Palmeiro was disturbed to hear that Orioles owner, Peter Angelos, had proposed that the Orioles play an exhibition game in Cuba. Though the State Department swiftly denied the request, the Palmeiros were still upset about it. "We left there 25 years ago because of what Castro stands for. We didn't believe in it. I don't see how I can go back. There is no way," Rafael said.

Rafael: Major League Statistical Data

YR	CLUB	G	AB	R	H	2B	3B	HR	RBI	BB	SO	AVG
1986	Cubs	22	73	9	18	4	0	3	12	4	6	.247
1987	Cubs	84	221	32	61	15	1	14	30	20	26	.276
1988	Cubs	152	580	75	178	41	5	8	53	38	34	.307
1989	Rang	156	559	76	154	23	4	8	64	63	48	.275
1990	Rang	154	598	72	191	35	6	14	89	40	59	.319
1991	Rang	159	631	115	203	49	3	26	88	68	72	.322
1992	Rang	159	608	84	163	27	4	22	85	72	83	.268
1993	Rang	160	597	124	176	40	2	37	105	73	85	.295
1994	Os	111	436	82	139	32	0	23	76	54	63	.319
1995	Os	143	554	89	172	30	2	39	104	62	65	.310
1996	Os	162	626	110	181	40	2	39	142	95	96	.289
1997	Os	158	614	95	156	24	2	38	110	67	109	.254

Chronology and Bio Stats

- Born September 24, 1964 in Havana, Cuba
- Mother: Maria Corrales Palmeiro; Father: José Palmeiro
- Brothers: Rick (January 22, 1962); Andy (June 19, 1967)
- Family left Cuba in 1971
- Grew up in Miami, Florida
- 1982, graduated from Miami Jackson High School
- June 7, 1982, selected by the New York Mets organization in eighth round of free-agent draft
- 1982–1985, attended Mississippi State University
- June 11, 1985, signed as first-round pick with the Chicago Cubs
- December 1985, married Lynne Walden
- 1987, called up to the major leagues
- 1988, became U.S. citizen
- 1988, ranked second in National League in batting; had twenty-game hitting streak; selected to play on the National League All-Star team
- December 5, 1988, traded to the Texas Rangers in an eight-player deal
- 1990, led the league with 191 hits in 154 games; was Texas Rangers MVP
- March 6, 1990, son Patrick born
- 1993, signed five-year, $30 million contract to play for the Baltimore Orioles
- January 22, 1995, son Preston born
- 1995 and 1996, hit career high 39 home runs each season
- 1996, batted in 142 runs
- May 12, 1996, hit 200th career home run
- 1997, hit 38 home runs; batted in 110 runs
- October 1997, won first Gold Glove award
- Currently: has homes in both Texas and Baltimore, Maryland

INDEX